Trans*

AMERICAN STUDIES NOW:
CRITICAL HISTORIES OF THE PRESENT

*Edited by Lisa Duggan and Curtis Marez*

Much of the most exciting contemporary work in American Studies refuses the distinction between politics and culture, focusing on historical cultures of power and protest on the one hand, or the political meanings and consequences of cultural practices, on the other. *American Studies Now* offers concise, accessible, authoritative, e-first books on significant political debates, personalities, and popular cultural phenomena quickly, while such teachable moments are at the forefront of public consciousness.

# Trans*

*A Quick and Quirky Account
of Gender Variability*

Jack Halberstam

UNIVERSITY OF CALIFORNIA PRESS

University of California Press, one of the most distin-
guished university presses in the United States, enriches
lives around the world by advancing scholarship in the
humanities, social sciences, and natural sciences. Its
activities are supported by the UC Press Foundation and
by philanthropic contributions from individuals and
institutions. For more information, visit www.ucpress.edu.

University of California Press
Oakland, California

Library of Congress Cataloging-in-Publication Data

Names: Halberstam, Judith, 1961– author.
Title: Trans* : a quick and quirky account of gender
    variability / Jack Halberstam.
Description: Oakland, California : University of
    California Press, [2018] | Includes bibliographical
    references.
Identifiers: LCCN 2017028209 (print) | LCCN 2017030891
    (ebook) | ISBN 978-0-520-96610-9 (ebook) |
    ISBN 978-0-520-29268-0 (cloth : alk. paper) |
    ISBN 978-0-520-29269-7 (pbk. : alk. paper)
Subjects: LCSH: Transgender people—Social conditions. |
    Gender identity—Social aspects.
Classification: LCC HQ77.9 (ebook) | LCC HQ77.9 .H35
    2018 (print) | DDC 306.76/8—dc23
LC record available at https://lccn.loc.gov/2017028209

Manufactured in the United States of America

26  25  24  23  22  21  20  19  18
10  9  8  7  6  5  4  3  2

*For Maca*

# CONTENTS

Conclusions
129

# OVERVIEW

## 1. TRANS*: WHAT'S IN A NAME?

Traces the historical legacies of categorization and classification as they pertain to the transgender body, with a focus on the importance of naming and un-naming. Classification systems connect with colonial strategies for knowing and governing.

*Pathologization · Legacies of Classification · Representation*

## 2. MAKING TRANS* BODIES

Surgeries both make and unmake trans* bodies. Not all trans* people have surgeries; not all surgeries are successful; some trans* people participate in the global market for cosmetic surgical tourism.

*Surgery · Bodily Architectures · Theories of Embodiment*

## 3. BECOMING TRANS*

Trans* children are the new frontier for rights, recognition, and medical intervention. This has favorable and unfavorable consequences for trans* activism.

*Trans* Child · Parenting · Trans* Defined*

## 4. TRANS* GENERATIONS

Trans* kinship across generations has been important in the
past, but currently parents have stepped into the role of
elders to younger generations of trans* teens. This has the
unfortunate impact of cutting trans* children off from trans*
history itself.

*Generational Struggle · Houses · Kinship*

## 5. TRANS* REPRESENTATIONS

Representations of trans* people in film and on TV have
tended to portray gender variant bodies as mad, bad, and
dangerous. This changed in the 1990s when we saw a slew of
films that addressed real struggles in trans* lives. Currently,
new generations of trans* activists contest older films in
favor of positive images, with sometimes disastrous effects.

*Cross-Generational Connections · Queer Energy/Anger · Representation*

## 6. TRANS* FEMINISMS

Feminisms and trans* activisms have historically been cast
as opposed, at odds, in conflict. The conflict is undeniable
and radical feminist critiques of trans* women have done
serious damage, but it may be time to look for grounds for
collaboration and solidarity.

*Feminism · Trans* Feminism · Solidarity*

## 7. CONCLUSIONS: MAKING AND UNMAKING BODIES

What can *The Lego Movie* tell us about building new
worlds, about architecture, and about trans* relations to
bodies and selves?

*Trans* Architecture · Legos · Elements · Piece of Resistance*

## ON PRONOUNS

How to play fast and loose with pronouns.

# PREFACE

You've got your mother in a whirl
She's not sure if you're a boy or a girl.

David Bowie, "Rebel, Rebel" (1974)

I started writing this book the day that David Bowie died. I found it strange to feel so sad about the loss of a person I had never met, but Bowie for me, as for so many people, represented the possibility of stretching beyond social norms and hackneyed cultural forms of expression and generic expectations. He embodied a deeply seductive and intelligent version of popular culture and managed to wed subversion to accessibility, rebellion to credibility, and transformation to performance. Over the course of a long and varied career in music and performance, David Bowie was able to sustain, with considerable vigor, a meaningful and lasting relation to musical experimentation, and he was able to articulate those experiments through bodily gestures and a series of ambiguously gendered personae. It is no accident that David Bowie's appeal, and many of his lyrics, were explicitly futuristic. His own gendered appearance—part man, part woman, part space alien—spoke of forms of life that extended far beyond the everyday understandings of "men" and "women" that circulated in the 1960s and 1970s when he began his journey into pop stardom.

Bowie is a perfect figure for the kinds of experiments in gender and embodiment that concern me in this book. Rather than giving a neat, chronologically ordered account of the emergence of transgender communities and trans visibility in the twenty-first century, I want to chart the undoing of certain logics of embodiment. When logic that fixes bodily form to social practice comes undone, when narratives of sex, gender, and embodiment loosen up and become less fixed in relation to truth, authenticity, originality, and identity, then we have the space and the time to imagine bodies otherwise.

Only a few months after Bowie's unexpected demise, another celebrity death shocked the world. Prince, the purple provocateur from Minneapolis, died too young of a drug overdose. Like Bowie, Prince had pioneered a gender-bending style that both emphasized his virtuosity and uniqueness and brought out a queerness, or sexual excess, and a transness, or gender ambiguity, that exceeds simple divisions between gay and straight or trans and cis and that offered access to complex, polyrhythmic worlds of love, lust, apocalypse, and heartbreak. Prince, a favorite icon for drag kings in the nineties and a figure so unclassifiable that for a while he refused a name and instead was known by a symbol, combined an authoritative ability to improvise and innovate with a playful tendency to flirt and seduce. For performers like Prince and Bowie, the opposing tendencies that our culture has placed in separate boxes were easily conjoined on behalf of, often, otherworldly productions of identity.

The sign that Prince used for a while to stand for his performance persona, a symbol commonly known as "the love symbol," combined the signs for man and woman. Prince used the symbol in an effort to part ways with his record label, Warner Bros., which, he felt, was exploiting him and his music in a way that could be called, he said, "slavery."[1] By using an unpronounceable symbol, Prince felt that he could interrupt the label's plan for squeezing the maximum amount of profit out of his work. By calling attention to the unjust ownership of Black music by white-run labels, and by recognizing that this ownership of Black culture extends through the gender-stabilizing insistence on naming and classification, Prince refused to obey the laws of gender, genre, or generic marketing. In his music, too, Prince sidestepped conventional gendered performances, and he inhabited a vocal range that veered abruptly from low growls to falsetto trills. Shifting and switching between styles, voices, soul, funk, rock, and punk, Prince likewise represents the gendered complexity to which, in the realm of popular culture, audiences are already attuned.

So, let Bowie and Prince, as well as Anohni or Jayne County, represent the kind of histories that gather under the sign of "Trans*." It is not a matter of whose gender is variable and whose is fixed; rather, the term "trans*" puts pressure on all modes of gendered embodiment and refuses to choose between the identitarian and the contingent forms of trans identity. With the ghosts of Bowie and Prince as our guides, we will go where trans* takes us, looking not for trans people (or people who have legally changed their sex) but for a politics of transitivity. Let's look at forms of gender, idioms of gender, gender practices and ask all the while how gender shifts and changes through all bodies and how it might be imagined in the future. In short, and as befits both of these eclectic performers, "let's dance."

# ONE

# Trans*

*What's in a Name?*

Whatever is not normative is many.

Eileen Myles, quoted in Ariel Levy,
"Dolls and Feelings" (2015)

Over the course of my lifetime I have called myself or been called a variety of names: queer, lesbian, dyke, butch, transgender, stone, and transgender butch, just for starters. Indeed, one day when I was walking along the street with a butch friend, we were called faggots! If I had know the term "transgender" when I was a teenager in the 1970s, I'm sure I would have grabbed hold of it like a life jacket on rough seas, but there were no such words in my world. Changing sex for me and for many people my age was a fantasy, a dream, and because it had nothing to do with our realities, we had to work around this impossibility and create a home for ourselves in bodies that were not comfortable or right in terms of who we understood ourselves to be. The term "wrong body" was used often in the 1980s, even becoming the name of a BBC show about transsexuality, and offensive as the term might sound now, it at least harbored an explanation for how cross-gendered people might experience embodiment: I, at least, felt as if I was in the wrong body, and there seemed to be no way out.

Today, young people who cross-identify are able to imagine themselves into other bodies, bodies that feel more true to who they are. And as times change, as medical technologies shift and develop, we also struggle to name the new "right-ish" bodies that emerge while continuing to work around the "wrong" bodies that remain. This chapter sifts through the changing protocols and rubrics for bodily identification over the past hundred years and asks, simply, what is in a name?

♀ ♀ ♀

Many a great novel begins with a name or identification of some sort—"Call me Ishmael."[1] Or, "My father's family name being Pirrip, and my Christian name Philip, my infant tongue could make of both names nothing longer or more explicit than Pip."[2] But also, "As Gregor Samsa awoke one morning from uneasy dreams he found himself transformed in his bed into an enormous insect."[3] And of course, "I, Saleem Sinai, later variously called Snotnose, Stainface, Baldy, Sniffer, Buddha and even Piece-of-the-Moon, had become heavily embroiled in Fate—at the best of times a dangerous sort of involvement."[4] Names establish character, lead into events, and create expectations. To be sure, there are also novels that begin in the absence of names: "I am an invisible man" and "Where now? Who now? When now?"[5] These non-naming flourishes challenge the idea of character and raise questions about the ability of naming to capture all the nuances of human identification. Indeed, one of the most lovable children's cartoons of all time, *Finding Nemo,* features a friendship between a clownfish, Nemo, whose name means "nobody" in Latin, and a blue fish, Dory, who can barely remember her own name from one moment to the next.⁶ The confusion that both Nemo and Dory sow leads not to a cozy lesson about who we "really" are but in fact makes the argument for learning to be part of a group, in part by challenging "proper" names. I offer these examples to make sense of the powerful nature of naming—claiming a name or refusing to and thus remaining unnameable. Indeed, this book uses the term "trans*," which I will explain shortly, specifically because it holds open the meaning of the term "trans" and refuses to deliver certainty through the act of naming.⁷

In a contemporary context, it is hard to imagine what it may have felt like to lack a name for one's sense of self. But only a few decades ago, transsexuals in Europe and the United States did not feel that there was a language to describe who they were or what they needed. Christine Jorgensen, heralded by historian Joanne Meyerowitz and others as "America's first transgender celebrity," wrote a letter to her parents in the 1950s telling them that in her "nature made a mistake."⁸ And in Radclyffe Hall's infamous novel about inversion, *The Well of Loneliness* (1928), the female-born protagonist, who calls herself Stephen, anguishes about her identity. Her governess, also an invert, tells her in a magnificent speech,

> You're neither unnatural, nor abominable, nor mad; you're as much a part of what people call nature as anyone else; only you're unexplained as yet—you've not got your niche in creation. But some day that will come, and meanwhile don't shrink from yourself, but face yourself calmly and bravely. Have courage; do the best you can with your burden. But above all be honourable. Cling to your honour for the sake of those others who share the same burden. For their sakes show the world that people like you and they can be quite as selfless and fine as the rest of mankind. Let your life go to prove this—it would be a really great life-work, Stephen.⁹

Hall used the term "misfit" for herself and called her hero, Stephen, an outlaw as well as an outcast and an invert, the word used in the early twentieth century in Europe and the United States to describe people in whom gender identity and sexual instincts have been turned around, such that a female-bodied person desiring another woman would be considered a male soul trapped in a female body and a male-bodied person harboring same-sex desires would be seen as a female soul trapped in a male body. The term "inversion" has a certain explanatory power in *The Well of Loneliness,* but only in that it names a disastrous betrayal of some putatively natural femininity. Until the middle of the last century, countless transgender men and women fell between the cracks of the classifications systems designed to explain their plight and found themselves stranded in unnameable realms of embodiment. Today we have an abundance of names for who we are and some people actively desire that space of the unnamable again. This book explains how we came to be trans* and why having a name for oneself can be as damaging as lacking one.

Naming, needless to say, is a powerful activity and one that has been embedded in modern productions of expertise and knowledge production. I have selected the term "trans*" for this book precisely to open the term up to unfolding categories of being organized around but not confined to forms of gender variance. As we will see, the asterisk modifies the meaning of transitivity by refusing to situate transition in relation to a destination, a final form, a specific shape, or an established configuration of desire and identity. The asterisk holds off the certainty of diagnosis; it keeps at bay any sense of knowing in advance what the meaning of this or that gender variant form may be, and perhaps most importantly, it makes trans* people the authors of their own categorizations. As this book will show, trans* can be a name for expansive forms of difference, haptic relations to knowing, uncertain modes of being, and the disaggregation of identity politics predicated upon the separating out of many kinds of experience that actually blend together, intersect, and mix. This terminology, trans*, stands at odds with the history of gender variance, which has been collapsed into concise definitions, sure medical pronouncements, and fierce exclusions.

The mania for the godlike function of naming began, unsurprisingly, with colonial exploration. As anyone who has visited botanical or zoological gardens knows, the collection, classification, and analysis of the world's flora and fauna has gone hand in hand with various forms of colonial expansion and enterprise. The seemingly rational and scientific project of collecting plant specimens from around the world and replanting them at home masks conquest with taxonomy, invasion with progress, and occupation with cultivation. But naming drifted quickly in the nineteenth century from plant life to human life; as many historians of sexuality have detailed, the terms that we now use to describe and explain gender and sexual variation were introduced into the language between 1869 and the first decade of the twentieth century.

Many theorists and historians have noted the way that expertise became a major component of early-industrialized societies. As large, complex social groups emerged at the end of the nineteenth century in Europe and the United States, having moved from agrarian to urban settings and from farm work to factory work, the systems of knowledge that tried to keep up with massive social changes produced experts in every field. There were time management experts who studied how to extract labor from bodies and machines as efficiently as possible.[10] Criminal anthropologists such as Cesare Lombroso measured heads and hands to argue that there were body types given over to crime and violence.[11] The

differences between men and women were codified and formal-
ized in relation both to certain types of work for working-class
women and to the household division into separate spheres for
bourgeois women. Ideas of racial identity that had long been
deployed within colonialism in order to justify brutal forms of rule
now became a part of the logic of governance and racial difference,
and racial categories, in turn, fed into the new understandings of
gender and sexuality that were circulating courtesy of doctors,
medical researchers, and the new discipline of psychoanalysis.
Having language for certain modes of desire had an enormous
impact on how people lived, loved, and hid or exposed themselves.
All of these efforts to classify human behavior emerged out of
and contributed to ongoing racial projects that held apart white
populations from populations of color; these "scientific" distinctions between normal and abnormal bodies lent support to white
supremacist projects that tried to collapse racial otherness into
gender variance and sexual perversion.

When it came to gender and sexuality, few eras were as turbu-
lent as the 1890s and the early decades of the twentieth century.
And while today Facebook famously offers you fifty-one ways of
identifying yourself on their site, a hundred years ago those categories were under rapid construction using the raw materials of
accelerated urbanization, diverse populations in small and dense
areas, and intensification of the desire to classify, know, and define.
So, rather than a great leap forward, our current profusion of classificatory options actually harks back to the early days of sexology, when doctors like Richard von Krafft-Ebing produced new,
expert knowledge on human sexual and gendered behavior. In
1886, Krafft-Ebing circulated a huge compendium of what he
called the "contrary sexual instinct," and in the table of contents
readers could find discussions on a multitude of erotic states, from

"Anthropophagy" to "Whipping of Boys," "Necrophilia" to "Larvated Masochism."[12] For Krafft-Ebing (writing before Freud had codified sexual instincts in relation to fixed orientations), the task was to document exhaustively the variety of forms within which the sexual instinct could be expressed. Of less interest to Krafft-Ebing was the articulation of a streamlined system opposing male to female and homo- to heterosexuality. Krafft-Ebing's work on gender and sexuality emerged at a time when Europe was engaged in a large-scale imperial orientation toward classification, collection, and expertise. Our current investments in the naming of all specificities of bodily form, gender permutations, and desire emerge from this period.

This project of exhaustive classification, a nineteenth-century practice that, as I have said, extended from botany to early anthropology to sexology, gave way in the twentieth century to the framing of the sexual and gendered body in relation to orientation, norms, and identity. Freud pushed back on nineteenth-century notions of an external frame that makes explicit the internal secrets of the body (this was at least one of the themes of criminal anthropology expressed by Lombroso and others) and argued for attention to the irrational, the unconscious, and the orientation of desire. Michael Foucault, in turn, refused the notion of an empirically verifiable set of orientations and argued that psychoanalysis produced the very concepts of bodily identity that it claimed to discover; and, he added, the production of the gendered and sexual body was co-orchestrated by the subject, who regulated himself in relation to social norms. The fiction of a gendered and sexual identity, Foucault proposed, took hold and became the reigning narrative of being in late twentieth-century life.[13]

Our current vocabularies combine an assortment of medical and vernacular terms—the medical terminology was produced in the last century and the vernacular terms have evolved alongside it as corrections, modifications, and, often, outright refusals. And so, we still occasionally use the medical word "homosexual" for same-sex desire, but more often we say "gay" or "lesbian"; we do use the term "transsexual" more often than "homosexual," but that is because transsexuals still are tethered in some way to medical technologies and services because they/we desire surgeries and hormones. And the term "transgender" has emerged in recent years as a way of collecting the many lived forms of transsexuality that include no-op transsexuals, no-hormones transsexuals, and others. The power of naming that has fallen to doctors and psychologists, social workers and academics, commands the authority of scientific inquiry and joins it to a system of knowledge that invests heavily in the idea that experts describe rather than invent. However, as we know from watching the slow implosion of seemingly "natural" systems from one hundred years ago, naming fixes bodies in time and space and in relation to favored social narratives of difference.

The terms homosexual/heterosexual and transsexual as well as other markers like man/woman, masculine/feminine, whiteness/blackness/brownness, are all historically variable terms, untethered in fixed or for that matter natural or inevitable ways to bodies and populations. While homosexuality tells at the same time the history of heterosexuality, and while women's histories are all too often absorbed by men's histories, transhirstory is a story waiting to be told. In an amusing commentary on this lost history, transgender artist Chris Vargas has created a Museum of Transgender Hirstory and Art (MOTHA: www.chrisevargas.com/motha/). This imaginary institution has the goal of "bringing a cohesive visual history of transgender culture into existence," using a framework that is deliberately perpetually "under construction." In this way, Vargas asks what it would mean to build a set of interlocking histories around people who regularly and sometimes deliberately fall out of the historical record.

"Words change depending upon who speaks them; there is no cure," writes Maggie Nelson in a more poetic intervention into this current confusion over gender-variant language. "The answer is not just to introduce new words (*boi, cis-gendered, andro-fag*) and then set out to reify their meanings (though obviously there is power and pragmatism here). One must also become alert to the multitude of possible uses, possible contexts, the wings with which each word can fly."[14] Seeing language in this way, as a shifting ecosystem within which words might fly, fall, or fail to convey their message, but also one within which words might hover over the multiplicity to which they point, relieves us of the mundane task of simply getting the name right.

We would do well to heed this lyrical warning against looking to stabilize fluctuations in meaning. If we seek to find in language an exhaustive catalogue of all human forms, we might stray into the kind of artificial production of multiplicity that informs the fifty-one ways to be a body offered us by Facebook. What do these terminologies represent in terms of the creation and collapse of contemporary systems of sex/gender definition? One of the first terms mentioned on Facebook is a relatively new one that signifies a person's exclusion from or rejection of gender categories: "agendered." An agendered person might be androgynous, gender fluid, gender neutral. The concept of being without a gender, however, is whimsical at best, since there are few ways to interact with other human beings without being identified with some kind of gendered embodiment. The concept of "agender," then, names a wish to be outside of gender norms, rather than the real experience of being so. Indeed, while liberal democracies cleave to the idea of gender neutrality or race blindness, it is very clear in these societies that historically situated differences are extremely important to name, study, recognize, and account for, if only because they provide histories of legally sustained hate and antipathy.

Other newish terms included in Facebook's "generous" range include "cis-gender," a relatively recent term now in widespread usage for people who have genders compatible with their genital forms. "Gender nonconforming," "gender questioning," and "neutrois"—people who fall outside of or who oppose the binary gender system—are more vernacular terms naming not only bodily identity but also the process of learning to live in a body (gender questioning). All of these terms have emerged within communities seeking for ways to name and explain their multiplicity: in other words, they are not medical terms or psychiatric terms produced in institutional contexts either to name disorders or to delimit a field of classification; rather, they are terms that emerge from trial and error, everyday usage, and political expediency. This might give us cause for optimism about the breakdown in classificatory regulations. And yet in fact, the older systems of classification have given way to vernacular systems without necessarily shifting the central and dominant binaries of race, class, gender, and sexuality. Rumors of the demise of hegemonic sex/gender systems, in other words, have been greatly exaggerated.

That said, one of the biggest innovations of the past two decades in relation to gendered expression indeed has been the production, circulation, and usage of just such a vernacular language for nonnormative gender and sexual expression. This emergence of new language signals the end of a period of medical/psychiatric control of the discourse and the beginning of a new paradigm within which people collaborate to name their understandings of contrary embodiment. This new period, as I will document in what follows, has produced rich and compelling narratives and accounts of the complex field of gendered and sexual expression. Perhaps nothing encapsulates these changes more succinctly than the increasingly common use of the term "they" for individuals who refuse to place themselves within a gender binary. Some people find this term to be ungainly given that is it a grammatical stretch because it maps a plural pronoun onto an individual body. Indeed, in a *New Yorker* article on Jill Soloway, the creator of the enormously successful TV comedy *Transparent,* Ariel Levy responds to Jill's challenge to "say 'they' and 'them' for all genders" by pointing out to her that "strict grammar forbids using a plural pronoun for a single person; it would sound crazy, for instance, to describe Soloway by saying, 'They are my favorite director.'"[15] Soloway pushes back, though, saying, "The language is evolving daily—even gender reassignment, people are now calling it gender confirmation!" Levy's skepticism wanes by the end of the article, when she asks Soloway's muse, queer poet Eileen Myles, whether, "as a poet, she struggled to refer to an individual person as 'they.' She said, 'It's not intuitive at all. But I'm obsessed with that part in the Bible when Jesus is given the opportunity to cure a person possessed by demons, and Jesus says, "What is your name?" And the person replies, "My name is legion." Whatever is not normative is many.' She liked the idea of a person containing more than one self, more than one gender."[16]

And the poet wins the day. What struck Levy, the journalist, as inelegant and ungrammatical strikes Myles as nonnormative and full of possibility. The use of the plural for the singular, the referencing of the many over the individual, contains within it, Myles implies, a small step toward utopia, a conjuring of collectivity in the place of individualism and recognition. We might add that genders only emerge in relation to other bodies and within multiply oriented and complex populations.

As the explosion of these terminologies suggests, the categories we use to understand the dynamic relations between and among pleasure, identification, social recognition, reproduction, and libidinal urges, not to mention parenthood, ability, national identity, age, and privacy, shift and change relatively quickly, and they do so under pressure from new forms of activism that pay careful attention to what we call ourselves, how we label others, and what falls into the domain of self-naming or slips into the dangerous territory of hate speech.

As this short book will show, however, vernacular forms of expression and definition are not necessarily less regulatory or less committed to norms than other modes of classification. While some strands of transgender activism have committed to the abolition of state regulation of the body (see, e.g., work by Dean Spade on administrative law, for example, or by Eric Stanley on prisons),[17] others have committed to a politics of recognition and participated in local and often futile and counterproductive quarrels over naming, language, and speech norms.

We can find one example of this last set of tensions between naming and being named in a local skirmish in San Francisco in the summer of 2014 when trans activists asked the owner of a queer bar called Trannyshack to change its name. The term "tranny," as the owner of Trannyshack, San Francisco–based drag queen Heklina (a.k.a. Stefan Grygelko), tried to explain in posts on Facebook and elsewhere, was not always understood as a hateful slur. The club began in 1996, and at that time "tranny" had the ring of a term of endearment—it was a diminutive, after all, like *kitten*, rather than a degrading pornographic term like *she-male*. Trannyshack was also a space often shared by gay men and transwomen and may have provided a meeting place for gay men who had, at some point in their lives, been marked by the term "sissy" and transwomen for whom gay club spaces were experimental and flexible. By 2014, two decades later, the term rang a false note and sounded to trans activists in the city like an insult. After heated debates on Facebook and elsewhere that involved public trans entertainers such as Vivian Bond and RuPaul (who defended the use of the term "tranny"), Heklina, fearing that she might be on the wrong side of history, changed the club's name to T-Shack. In a statement, Heklina wrote: "I am in the business of (hopefully) entertaining people.... Also, on a purely business level, I don't want to be viewed as archaic, out of step with the times, like an ostrich with my head in the sand."[18] Heklina cites both business and pleasure in her justification for the name change. But she also acknowledges that certain modes of naming gender-transitive bodies might be "archaic" as we enter a new era of sex/gender norms.

These kinds of conflicts over naming and slang are situated differently, however, by LaMonda Horton Stallings, a Black cultural studies scholar who argues that we might see a different side to this debate if we situate "uses of 'tranny' by transgender individuals within a history of blackness and language rather than a history of gender."[19] Turning to the use of the term "tranny" in the TV show *RuPaul's Drag Race,* and referencing RuPaul's own defense of the term, Stallings proposes that when RuPaul claims the term "tranny," s/he does so in relation not to white transgender histories but within Black histories of gender variance that remain distinct from mainstream narratives of transgender emergence.[20] Indeed, Stallings proposes, the term tranny "is specifically linked within a history and culture of sex work that transgender erases" and that it has meaning as a "monetary term" for sex workers who use it transactionally in the context of selling a specific kind of sex.[21] Stallings makes clear that mainstream narratives of transgenderism mostly presume white bodies and white histories of sex and gender and she proposes that we pay careful attention to the very different ways that sex and gender signify for trans people of color.

As this quarrel indicates, the answer to the question "What's in a name?" is "Everything!" But when we argue over terminology, are we ignoring structures? In other words, is the contestation over naming a distraction from much bigger problems that are not linguistic but systemic or institutional? Then again, is the linguistic actually already a symptom of these large systems that both fix us and allow us to imagine ourselves as free? While the case of the T-Shack provides a real-world example of a fight over names and language that reveals much about shifting gender norms, I now want to take a long detour through a humorous cinematic example of a contestation over words that may open on to more complicated understandings of naming, claiming, speech, silence, and protest.

The wacky archive of Monty Python gives us lots of ammunition to consider the stakes in new wars about words. Their feature film *The Life of Brian*, for example, tells the wonderfully absurd story about a mistaken messiah, the eponymous Brian, who was born next door to Jesus Christ and who stumbles into a political action by the People's Front of Judea and ends up on the wrong end of Roman law.[22] The film, a satire as well as a goofy critique of religion and orthodoxies in general, provides lots of fodder for thinking about how we continue to cast about for political direction in the middle of global meltdown. It also offers much in the way of jokes in Latin, men in skirts, and women in beards. The film, in fact, presents its audience (when it came out in 1979 as well as now) with a perfect analysis of what can go wrong in political struggles (infighting, unimaginative activist group names, too much talking, hopeless actions against the occupying forces), what can go right (not much), and what battles over language are worth fighting.

In one priceless scene, Brian (played by Graham Chapman), having been sent by the People's Front of Judea to participate in his first anti-imperialist graffiti action, begins to paint "Romanes Eunt Domus"—Romans Go Home in Latin—on a wall.[23] He is just finishing up when a centurion (John Cleese) stops him. Sure that he is done for, Brian trembles in the shadow of the Roman solder. But what follows is a Latin lesson in which Brian is reminded that the plural of Romans is *Romani;* he is then forced to conjugate the Latin verb for "to go" and to find the imperative form of the third person plural, *ite.* Finally, Cleese, the perfect Latin teacher, makes Brian rewrite *Domus* in the locative, as *Domum.* Corrected version: "Romani Ite Domum"! As punishment for his bad Latin, he is told to write the phrase 100 times on the walls of the Roman city.

This is a hilarious scene that draws its humor, and its allegorical force, from the impression that many schoolchildren of a certain generation (ahem ... my generation) received about Latin: namely, that it was a "dead" language mostly used to instruct youngsters in the rules of grammar and, by implication, all kinds of other useless rules that, along with their irrational "exceptions," had to be followed. For students of Latin in Europe in the 1960s and 1970s, content was subordinate to form—even in a book like Caesar's *Gallic Wars* ("All of Gaul is divided into three parts ... ," etc.), a text brimming with information about imperialism, domination, cunning leadership, political corruptions, territorial gains, protonationalism, and so forth. In my youth we read for pure translation, never discussing the actual content of the text.

Cleese's centurion in *The Life of Brian* takes this joke to an extreme by catching an anti-imperialist activist in the act of defacing Roman property and using the opportunity to instruct him in the rules of the imperial language. With a sneaky nod to Fanon, the Pythons are able to remind us that imperial and colonial domination occurs through language and that although the war of words might seem to be happening at the level of content and meaning, actually it is conducted by means of form or grammar. Getting the grammar right, in *The Life of Brian* as elsewhere, means linking sense to the arbitrary rules of the oppressor class. But the allegory of domination and resistance does not end there. In his fervor to protect the rightness of Roman rule, Cleese not only instructs the reluctant revolutionary in how to address Rome; he also gives him an opportunity, disguised as a punishment—he tells him to write the offensive phrase 100 times. By the time he has finished, Brian has covered every square inch of the Roman walls with the words Romans Go Home! Or, in perfect Latin: Romani Ite Domum!

This episode reminds us that sometimes we really cannot see the forest for the trees, the Roman Empire for the cheery centurions, or the site of linguistic domination for the miscellaneous slurs directed at marginal subjects. In queer communities today, while we fight about words like "tranny," worry about being triggered, and "call each other out" for our supposed microcrimes of omission/inclusion/slang, we are, like the People's Front of Judea, trying to fight power by battling over the relations between signifiers and signifieds while leaving the structures of signification itself intact. But the episode also makes clear that punishment can lead to protest: Brian's punishment allows him to complete the activist mission that he was sent to carry out in the first place.

No doubt, this whole book could draw wisdom from antic episodes in Monty Python, but before we succumb to such a tempting idea, let's circle back around to the topic at hand. What has happened in the last few decades to prompt such an extensive overhaul of our understanding of and language for gendered embodiment? And how have people responded to new definitions of sex and the gendered body? In this book, I will try to narrate various experiences of transitive gender as they range across the human life span. Recognizing that, in this era of increased longevity, the experience and meaning of gendered embodiment and of sex and pleasure can change radically over time, *Trans** separates out gender ambiguity in the child from adolescent crises over embodiment and from trans* issues related to parenting, having children, growing old, and even dying.

In the last decade, public discussions of transgenderism have increased exponentially. What was once regarded as an unusual or even unfortunate disorder has become an accepted articulation of gendered embodiment as well as a new site for political activism. How did a stigmatized identity become so central to U.S. and European articulations of self and other? What fuels the continued fascination with transgender embodiment, and how has the recognition of its legitimacy changed current gender protocols in the United States? What is the history of gender and how does it sit alongside histories of sexuality, race, ability, and health?

Whether it comes in the form of Preferred Gender Pronouns (PGP) or even new classifications of gender identity (agender, androgynous, cis-gender), the visibility of transgender must be seen as part of a larger shift in habits and customs around classification, naming, and inhabiting of the human body. While new gender protocols as expressed on Facebook and in other forms of social media seem to register advancement, flexibility, and even a decentering of normative gendering, increased flexibility with regard to gender may function as a part of new regulatory regimes. *Trans*\* pays attention to the ebb and flow of regulation and innovation, governance, and experimentation.

In addition to placing shifts and changes in trans identities firmly within a matrix of gender and sexuality identities and practices, *Trans*\* will argue that new visibility for any given community has advantages and disadvantages, liabilities and potentialities. With recognition comes acceptance, with acceptance comes power, with power comes regulation. New articulations of the experience of gender ambiguity, in other words, will make lots of people's lives easier (transgender adults, but also their parents or their children, their friends, their lovers), but it could also have unforeseen consequences in terms of exposing people who were passing in one gender or another to new forms of scrutiny and speculation.

As far as statistics go, and for some of us that is not very far, some estimates reckon that there are currently 1.4 million transgender people in the United States.[24] Many transgender people report having been the victims of harassment and bullying, with transwomen in general and transwomen of color in particular being the most likely targets of violence and exclusion. In addition, HIV rates for transwomen are very high.[25] Many transgender people, reports suggest, have attempted suicide.[26] While reported physical abuse of transgender people is high, we have to factor gender, race, and class into these analyses. Poverty, sex work, and race remain significant variables in determining which transgender individuals are regularly subject to violence on account of their gender expression. This book will try to grapple with some hard questions about violence, vulnerability, gender presentation, and the psychological impact of transphobia.

At the same time, it is noteworthy that in May 2013 the *Diagnostic and Statistical Manual of Mental Disorders (DSM-V)* removed the category of transgender from its list of bodily disorders, replacing it with the term "gender dysphoria."[27] The movement of transgender identification from pathology to preference, from a problematic fixation to a reasonable expression of self, follows the route from problem to social identity that has described the history of homosexuality in the twentieth century. As with LGB identities, trans identities now qualify as both new sites for the expression of liberal acceptance and new platforms for demands for recognition. Whether gender transitivity can also offer a critique of contemporary modes of power and empowerment remains to be seen.

Monty Python certainly thought that trans identities offered a platform for more ostentatious forms of critique. In another chapter from *The Life of Brian*, the liberation fighters who are opposing the Romans discuss both their right to organize in the face of imperialist brutality and the importance of representing the broadest possible constituency.[28] Reg (Cleese) and Francis (Michael Palin) are making the case for their right as men to oppose the ruling order. "Or women," interjects Stan (Eric Idle). "Or women," the others concede. As another round of activist statements and pronouncements begins, Stan continues to interject "or women ... or sisters" whenever men or brothers are mentioned. Finally Reg, irritated by these annoying add-ons to what he considers to be the main agenda, turns on Stan and asks him why he is so obsessed suddenly with the rights of women. Stan plays the Pythonesque role of "interrupter," where the interruption, rather than forestalling the discussion, takes it off somewhere else entirely—"and now for something completely different." In this case, the different place is the transgender desire harbored by a male-bodied person, Stan, to become female-bodied Loretta and to bear children. Loretta claims that it is her right as a man to have babies and that Reg is "oppressing" her by denying her this right. While the defensive response to this text might be to claim that it makes light of the experience of transgender women, a trans* reading could open the sequence up to a new rendering of transgenderism as a desire for forms of embodiment that are necessarily impossible and yet deeply desired, all at once. Even though Loretta's sex reassignment will never allow her to have babies, the People's Front of Judea affirms her right to fight for the right to have babies because this demand for the impossible "symbolizes" the anti-imperial struggle to which they have committed. Loretta's trans desire, indeed, represents both the impossibility and possibilities of all forms of embodiment.

Returning to LaMonda Horton Stallings's book *Funk the Erotic: Transaesthetics and Black Sexual Cultures,* Stallings uses the term "trans" as a verb and, building on Susan Stryker's idea of "transing," claims: "I trans black literary studies and sexuality studies to demonstrate how black communities' deployment of funk provides alternative knowledge about imagination and sexuality."[29] Funk, according to this system of meaning making, does not observe binaries proper to white humanism like the sacred and the profane, the erotic and the pornographic, work and pleasure; instead, Stallings deploys a mechanism of sex/power/profanity that she names "funky erotixxx" to refuse and depart from the sexual morality invested in neat distinctions, in order to pursue a transaesthetics that is not invested in a singular reality.

*Trans\** will survey current representations of transgender people alongside new laws designed to recognize transgenderism as a protected category. It will provide potted histories alongside social analysis, and it will speculate about the future of (trans) gender even while it describes how transgenderism has long been situated as a site of futurity and utopian/dystopian potential. A popular T-shirt from the queer crafts collective Otherwild proposes that "The Future is Female." Is it? Or is the future genderless, gender variable, gender optional, gender hacked—or none of the above?[30] We may not know what gender or transgender will become in the next few decades, but we can certainly account for its past, its present, and its potentiality.

# TWO

# Making Trans* Bodies

There are the facts of what happened but, like a body,
the story is in parts.

Thomas Page McBee, *Man Alive* (2014)

In 2016 at the grand old age of fifty-four, having lived in my boy-ish but female body for over half a century, I made a big decision: I wanted top surgery. Nearly a hundred years ago when British medical researcher Michael Dillon had what was probably the first top surgery, he did so almost by accident. After being hospi-talized for something else, according to biographer Pagan Kennedy, Dillon heard that a plastic surgeon was in residence at the hospital. Plastic surgeons were a rarity at this time and were still "regarded as quacks."[1] Nonetheless, Dillon leaped at the chance that fate had thrown his way and asked the surgeon to give him a double mastectomy. Nowadays, plastic surgeons court transgender patients, and some transgender people can get most or all of their procedures paid for through medical insurance.

I called to make my appointment with a surgeon recommended by a friend. Doctor Li was not someone who specialized in trans-gender medicine, but he was known to be very good at what he did. His receptionist asked what kind of procedure I wanted.

I paused. "Top surgery," I said. She didn't miss a beat. "No problem, hon." she answered, "I'll need your birth name, and then later, after the surgery, we can call you by your chosen name."

The clinic was bustling with women when I arrived. Butt implants seemed to be flavor of the month, but the woman who checked me in said that breast enhancement was the bread-and-butter procedure at the clinic. Top surgeries, though not uncommon, were not their everyday fare. Doctor Li apologized for having to ask me to provide a note from a therapist confirming that I suffered from "gender dysphoria" and needed the surgery for psychological reasons. He also said that he wished some of his other patients, young women, say, who wanted breast enlargements, would speak to someone before making such drastic changes to their bodies.

The day of my surgery, I arrived with my partner. Other transgender people have reported being subjected to scorn from the medical staff they encounter. There is nothing worse than being judged by people who are about to work on your body while you are under anesthesia. I experienced none of this, however; the women who cared for me were kind and understanding and nonjudgemental, and Doctor Li was calm and reassuring. "Why did you become a plastic surgeon?" I asked him moments before going under. "I always wanted to be an architect," he answered. "And plastic surgery allows me to build structures out of flesh."

Some people might have found this response odd, but Doctor Li's answer thrilled me. It only raised my confidence in his abilities and in his understanding of me, and my body. Together we were building something in flesh, changing the architecture of my body forever. The procedure was not about building maleness into my body; it was about editing some part of the femaleness that currently defined me. I did not think I would awake as a new self, only that some of my bodily contours would shift in ways that gave me a different bodily abode.

Indeed, one strand of trans* studies has insisted on this shift from the idea of embodiment as being housed in one's flesh to embodiment as a more fluid architectural project. Lucas Crawford, for example, writes beautifully about architectures of stone and flesh that determine, imprint, and shape the selves that move through them. Crawford pushes back on the concept of ownership implied in the conventional equation of bodies with homes in transgender studies and instead thinks of embodiment as a series of "stopovers" in which the body is lived as an archive rather than a dwelling, and architecture is experienced as productive of desire and difference rather than just framing space.[2] My surgery was one such stopover, my body is one such archive.

The desire to cross genders or change sex actually has a very long history, and we can easily find figures in historical archives who passed for their whole adult lives as men or women despite having been born into bodies they felt the need to repudiate. Books have been written on figures such as the French spy Chevalier d'Éon (1728–1810) and Catalina de Erauso (1592–1650), the so-called "lieutenant nun."[3] De Erauso began her life in a convent in Spain but escaped from the nunnery by wearing men's clothing, and then sailed to the Americas and engaged in many exploits, some militaristic, some criminal, some romantic. Chevalier d'Éon lived half his life as a man and then began wearing women's clothing, claiming to have been born female. Then there was Juana Aguilar, a hermaphrodite who, accused of unnatural acts with women in 1803 in Guatemala, was subjected to multiple medical examinations to determine whether she was male, female, both, or neither. The doctor appointed by the court of law to examine Aguilar, Narciso Esparragosa y Gallardo, concluded that she was "sexually neutral, like some bees."[4] In an important article about Aguilar, historian María Elena Martínez noted the incompleteness of the historical record, the impossibility of reading "truth" in the fragments that one finds there, and the inapplicability of contemporary models of sex and gender to historical figures, warning in general against applying terms like "gay," "lesbian," and "transgender" or "intersex" to figures from other eras. "The act of mapping a category onto subjects who may not have recognized the practices, lifestyles, notions of body and self, and so forth that it references," she writes, "aligns itself with a genealogy of power—one that imposes, distorts, or forecloses certain desires, identifications, and experiences. It can also entail missing an opportunity to discover in the past human possibilities and imaginings that were suppressed or left unfulfilled but that can provide guidance in the present for creating better worlds in the future."[5] This is a beautiful passage and a subtly nuanced proposal for how to go about historicizing ambiguous bodies.

While definitions of "homosexuality" eventually dropped the narrative of inversion, by which a lesbian was considered a man trapped in a woman's body and a gay man was thought to be a woman trapped in a man's body, this idea of one kind of gendered self encased within the other was the dominant expression of transsexual selfhood in the mid–twentieth century. Indeed, Michael Dillon, the British doctor I mentioned above, who is sometimes referred to as the "first transsexual man" due to his experiments with hormones and surgery in the 1930s and 1940s, used this narrative of being born into the wrong body to plead for medical interventions to ease the plight of the transsexual. Dillon also made an early attempt to separate out transsexual manhood from lesbian masculinity in a 1946 book titled *Self: A Study in Endocrinology and Ethics.*[6] The book was the first sustained attempt to identify transsexuality as a specific medical and psychological condition, one that could not be changed through therapy, that was not the same as lesbianism, and that required surgical and hormonal interventions.

Likening transsexuals to wounded soldiers back from World War One, Dillon argued that a medical response to transsexuality was a moral obligation. According to his biographer Pagan Kennedy, "In *Self,* Dillon became one of the first scholars in the world to work out a classification system for gender identity and sexual desire."[7] Some two decades before Harry Benjamin became the preeminent expert on sex change procedures, Dillon used the terminology of transsexuality and treated himself with hormones. Having a way of describing himself was helpful to Dillon, but more than that, he said, it also saved his life.

By the 1930s and 1940s when trans men like Michael Dillon and transwomen like Danish artist Lili Elbe experimented with hormones and surgery, there were clearly defined transsexual populations who did not simply want same-sex partners but who wanted to change their sex. Even so, the history of transsexuality has been hard to tell and transsexuals have often lived lives secretly and in hiding; many have not been able to access or afford medical assistance, and others may not have known where to turn even if they had the resources. While the terminology of transsexuality and transgenderism was central to the quest for medical interventions in the twentieth century, its power to recognize and locate a certain relation to the body has somewhat waned in a world where we confront the incomplete project of "sex change." Hormones have been extremely effective in allowing transgender men and women to pass, but "bottom" surgeries for the transformation of genitalia remain unsatisfactory for some men and women who choose to forgo them altogether.[8] For this and other reasons, the term "transgender" names a wide array of bodies with varying relations to cross-gender identification; I believe that the term "trans\*," which I use in this book, more accurately captures the provisional nature of sex reassignment. In this chapter and elsewhere in the book, I tend to privilege female to male transitions, transmale perspectives and theorizations, and the experiences of trans\* masculine subjects. This is not ideal, but it may be that trans\* embodiment is more different than similar for transgender men and women. While I would like to keep the focus equally on transgender women and men, my particular biography and my academic background tend to draw me to the trans\* masculine material.

While current understandings of transgender and transsexual bodies seem to emerge out of medical research, much broader frameworks have contributed to both the stability and the instability of current gender protocols. In some contexts, gender-ambiguous bodies have been swept into colonial logics of difference, even though they might have been understood differently prior to conquest. For example, in indigenous communities throughout the Americas, the split between male and female, homo and hetero, trans and cis-, was imposed by a settler-colonial logic of rule and did not necessarily correspond to existing divisions within these societies. As ethnographer and historian Scott Morgensen argues, "Memories and practices of discrepant sexual cultures among Indigenous peoples and peoples of color persistently trouble the white settler logics of sexual modernity."[9] In other words, the logic that seems so inevitable in contemporary U.S. contexts has been imposed and disputed in other times and places, and the category of trans* carries the marks of all of these earlier contestations over embodiment and its meanings.

In contemporary society, the ambiguity of anyone's gender functions less as a marker of aberration and more as a sign of the loosening restrictions on sexuality and gender for certain subjects. Thus, the colonial power to name has shifted away from the general management of gender-ambiguous bodies in Euro-American contexts and toward a more global production of power. Now, therefore, the colonial control over naming and explaining different forms of embodiment falls less to medicine and more to political organizations committed to the project of identifying and remedying transphobia and homophobia globally. These groups, needless to say, must first sculpt the very different systems of gender and identification they find in other countries into politically retrogressive models and then offer solutions to them. We will look at examples of this later in the chapter.

The more recent emphasis on *sexual and gender diversity* represents both a break with nineteenth- and twentieth-century concepts of classification, norms, and identity and a new mode of social control that continues the social project that classification and normative regulation began. The profusion of gendered identities that characterizes large urban populations in Europe and the United States in particular in the twenty-first century can be read as a breaking away from binary ideals, but, as the European theorist Paul Preciado shows, it can also be situated within new biomedical and pharmaceutical systems of bodily manipulation and control.[10] Preciado's work on the pharmaco-pornographic regimes of management of desire and identity proposes that terms like masculinity, femininity, heterosexuality, and homosexuality, not to mention transgenderism, are all

propped up and ultimately rendered meaningless, in the contemporary context, by flows of pharmaceutical enhancement—
Viagra, contraception, hormones, recreational drugs, pain pills,
and antidepressants—that reconfigure bodily identity through
molecular and chemical interventions rather than by investing
in notions of psychological or physiological health. Accordingly,
we need to place transgenderism firmly within new biopolitical
regimes where bodies are not simply the effect of performativity
or social constructions or gender ideologies but also repositories
for new chemical scripts in which bodies can be energized or
quieted, made fertile or infertile, awakened or numbed, made to
feel more or to feel less. These new scripts work from the inside
out and cannot be read and sorted in terms of identities and
morphologies. Instead, they produce embodiment as a portal for
the mixing of hormones, pain pills, antidepressants, mood ele-
vators, pain suppressants, libido enhancers, blood thinners, sleep
aids, diet aids, disease barriers, and anti-aging supplements.
The trans\* body within such a system names the desire for and
the results of a drug cocktail as much as it articulates a deeply
felt sense of being in the wrong flesh bag.

Massive shifts in the meaning of embodiment do not happen
overnight; rather, they accrue meaning over time, incrementally
but decisively. The kinds of shifts in the organization and meaning of the gendered body that Preciado narrates in his 2013 book
*Testo Junkie* have only recently reached a breaking point that
makes their effects visible within the culture at large. Because we
tend to need proof that tectonic shifts have occurred before we
declare the end or the start of a new paradigm, we are drawn to
bodies that seem new or different in ways that are visualizable
and verifiable. In the late nineteenth and early twentieth century,
masculine women and male dandies provided visual markers of

irreversible shifts in the meaning of the gendered body within new forms of capitalism. The dandy and the aristocratic butch both modeled new investments in bodily comportment, style, and wealth, and in the process they flouted the limits of gender norms even as they depended on new practices of consumer capitalism to do so. In the late twentieth and early twenty-first century, the transgender body performs a similar function—whether it manifests in the circulation and use of hormones or in new narratives of selfhood, the figure of transgender embodiment is central to numerous emergent narratives of self and other, being and becoming.

Preciado's narrative of a body that submits both ecstatically and anxiously to the effects of pharmaceutical manipulation traces a long arc from fifteenth-century witchcraft to midwifery, from the first uses of contraception to the discovery of hormones. Similarly, the narrative of flesh in the grip of various systems of pleasure and pain administered by pills dovetails with other narratives about the raced body, the classed body, the perfect body, and the disabled body. These ideological matrices impede and enable the flows of meaning, cultural expression, desire, and pain as they make their way into the body and then find their way out in aesthetic, political, social, and gestural expressions. Leaning more toward a Deleuzian understanding of the body as a liquid set of dynamics than toward either a Freudian concept of the hydraulic functions of repression or a Foucauldian insistence on the propulsive trajectory of power through flesh,[11] Preciado flips the terms of bodily identity away from surfaces (secondary sex characteristics, for example) and toward depths (molecular composition and decomposition), away from fragmentation (Freudian stages) and toward flow (the passage of chemicals through the organism), away from fictions of identity and toward a disarticulation of parts not only from wholes but even from other parts.

No one really knows what the long-term effects of taking hormones will be for transgender people. And so, while narratives like *Testo Junkie* thrill to the experience of shooting up testosterone and feeling the relatively quickly visible effects of masculinization, there are fewer narratives that tell us about male balding for men or waning libido for transwomen and other less visible signs and less desirable effects of long-term hormone use for transsexual men and women. Fewer still think about the shifts and changes in the trans\* body alongside the shifts and changes that buffet all bodies as they move through the roller coaster changes of adolescence, the indignities of aging, the painful processes of disease, the body-altering experiences of pregnancy, and so on. Maggie Nelson, one of the few writers to explore this contested terrain, compares her preparation for pregnancy to her partner's experiences with hormones and top surgery: "On the surface, it may have seemed as though your body was becoming more and more 'male,' mine more and more 'female.' But that's not how it felt on the inside. On the inside we were two human animals undergoing transformations beside each other, bearing each other loose witness. In other words, we were aging."[12] A few ideas emerge here: The feeling of the body as experienced from the inside can sometimes be at odds with appearance or external features. Also, the notion of change as a side-by-side process of transformation pushes back on the tendency to represent trans\* embodiment as unique and exceptional. Finally, the idea of bearing "loose witness" beautifully captures not just the experience of partnering with a trans\* person but the experience of partnering in general.

While Maggie's partner, Harry, experiences his top surgery alongside a caring and attentive witness, earlier trans\* people would have experienced their medical procedures with much trepidation and very much alone. Early experiences with sex reassignment surgery, as recorded by transsexual writers and memoirists, were quite gruesome and had mixed results. Michael Dillon records only satisfaction with his mastectomy, but of course the technology would not have been available at that time to construct a male-looking chest. Einar Wegener, on the other hand, a Danish painter who in 1930 sought medical assistance to become Lili Elbe, died one year later after a botched surgery. (The recent film based on this case, *The Danish Girl,* treats the surgery in a very oblique way and minimizes its risk.) And while contemporary surgeries, whether carried out by surgeons who specialize in transgender care or by plastic surgeons, are generally much more effective, there is no simple medical procedure that can seamlessly transform a female body into a male one or vice versa. Instead of focusing solely on hormones, on the one hand, or surgical interventions, on the other, we should probably pay closer attention to the topic of trans* health as it extends beyond the procedures for sex reassignment surgery.[13]

In an ethnography of transsexual surgeries and treatments, J. R. Latham centralizes surgery and examines the management of trans male bodies by medical professionals, offering a labile, versatile account of the multiplicity of trans experience. Arguing that all too often medical frameworks produce rather than treat, diagnose rather than observe, and fix rather than care for transgender bodies, Latham attempts to intervene in the medical protocols that govern and manage gender-variant subjects.[14] This study by Latham reminds us that, in an era when plastic surgery requests for non-transgendered people go unquestioned by medical professionals, transgender subjects continue to be held to unreasonable standards in terms of proving and demonstrating their emotional and mental stability.

Latham provides a clear and thorough appraisal of shifting understandings of trans bodies in U.S., European, and Australian culture and changing protocols of treatment within psychiatric and surgical facilities. Latham's main points are as follows: First, transgenderism both in queer theory and in medical practice has been streamlined into a singular phenomenon canceling out the wide range of experiences, of trans men in particular. Second, Latham argues, correctly I believe, that sexuality and the sexual practices of trans bodies have been underdescribed, if not simply ignored. David Valentine argued something similar a decade ago in his ethnography of the emergence of the transgender category in mostly trans-feminine contexts.[15] Existing scholarship has tended to ignore the sexual practices of trans men and women partly because of the voyeuristic attention directed in mass culture at the surgically made genitalia of trans people and partly due to a sense that transgender and transsexual identities are primarily experienced and produced as a gendered phenomenon rather than as part of a sexual practice. Third, Latham asks his readers to view sex and gender and sexuality as "ontologically multiple and mutually constituting." This goal obviously clashes with earlier models that demanded recognition for gender-variant bodies separate from sexual practices and relationships. Finally, using analytics drawn from Science and Technology Studies (STS), Latham proposes that we "rethink reality," particularly the realities that are produced to correspond to the centering of cis-gendered bodies and experiences.

It is this last argument that resonates for those of us who have focused our work on representation and the aesthetic regimes within which transgender realities are forged and denied. As I hope to demonstrate in this book, over the past century trans* bodies have been cast as unreal, inauthentic, and aberrant. This leads some activists to argue strenuously for the recognition of transgender and transsexual lives as real and true, but these claims tend to locate certain privileged trans* bodies (privileged in terms of race and class) as deserving while abandoning other trans* bodies and trans experiences to vulnerability and criminalization. Better, then, as Latham puts it, to invest in the refusal of "reality" from the position of the trans* body. Latham's work, indeed, argues for the recognition of the multiple realities that "hang together" within and in relation to the transgender body; and through a canny critique of "common sense realism," he provides a clear model for situating the trans body and its multiplicities. In the most basic terms, Latham explains how and why transgender people (here specifically trans men), rather than doctors, should be the arbiters and crafters of the multiple meanings of the trans body.

In other words, to the extent that trans* bodies are subject to psychiatric scrutiny for the choices people may make about body modification, it should only be for the same reasons that other non/trans bodies fall into at-risk categories. That is, while currently non/transgender men and women do not have to undergo psychiatric evaluation before having any kind of cosmetic surgery, unless there are other indicators of mental instability, so transgender men and women should be able to elect body modifications without psychiatric evaluation unless they too exhibit unstable behaviors. These seem like obvious claims to make within the marketplace of medical treatment, but, as so many trans* men and women testify in relation to their experiences with surgery, it is not at all the prevailing wisdom

A 2005 film 2005 by Daniel Peddle titled *The Aggressives,* which looks at masculine-defined people living in female bodies, provides insight into the necessity of broader understandings of trans* health care. *The Aggressives* focused on a group of transgender/butch Puerto Rican and Black "studs" in New York City, following them for a period of five years. The film, a fairly conventional talking-heads documentary, did not circulate widely at the time of its release, but it remains an important account of the very different experiences of gender variance for men and women of color and how those experiences intersect with regimes of health, criminali-zation, and discipline; it also offers a significantly different narrative from mainstream accounts. Calling themselves "aggressives," these trans* men readily distinguish themselves from both "women" and "transsexuals," and they talk about their sexual practices, their early childhood experiences, their relationships, their work lives. But they also discuss their relation to the law, to drug cultures, to money, poverty, and hardship, as well as their very negative experi-ences with the medical world and their complete lack of social support.

Over the course of the five years, one aggressive has an unex-plained hysterectomy, one goes to jail, one joins the army and then goes AWOL when commissioned to go to Iraq, one struggles to keep a job and does drugs. Some have children, some live with their parents. Being trans*, this documentary shows, for young people of color can simply mean more surveillance, more punish-ment, less health care. For example, one trans* character tracked by the film, Rjai, an African American, goes to the hospital for some unusual bleeding, and after being examined they are given a hysterectomy. They are not informed as to why they have had their uterus removed or what the diagnosis of the bleeding might have been. This episode highlights a very different relationship between the trans* subject and medical technology than the one that is often highlighted in relation to transsexuality. Here it is the history of the sterilization of Black women and Latinas that haunts the transgender body, not the history of sex changes. Unwittingly, *The Aggressives* shows that trans* embodiment and its treatment within various institutional settings cannot be separated out from the complex constellation of social pressures that converge on Black and Latino/a bodies in the United States. It reminds us of the futility of discrete analysis, and of the importance of what Rod Ferguson calls "queer of color critiques," which bind studies of sexuality and gender to considerations of class and race.[16] The documentary also marks the whiteness of the category "transgender" and implies that other terms exist in other communities and that these other terms indicate the function of gender in relation to a specific set of life experiences.

Indeed, Riley Snorton's ground-breaking account of the history of Black trans* bodies, *Black on Both Sides,* offers a quite different frame for race and gender than those that situate Christine Jorgensen and others as media celebrities. Snorton, using rarely combined archives of fugitive slave accounts, sexology, journalism, and film, offers the term "fungibility" to think about these other epistemological frames. Snorton argues that the concept of fungibility might give us access to the ways in which blackness overlaps with the instability of gender identity, thereby rewriting both the history of race *and* the history of transgenderism. The term "fungibility," relating to the nonspecific nature of certain forms of commodification, can also be applied, according to Snorton, to "multiple orders of interchangeability within blackness."[17] If, as Hortense Spillers has argued, the black body was "ungendered" by capture and exchange,[18] then, Snorton proposes, this ungendering gives access to both narratives and methods of fugitivity and it marks gender instability as part of the history of blackness itself. In other words, the mutability of gender definition as it was applied across white and black bodies in the nineteenth century gives evidence of the instability within identity categories that Black fugitives were able to harness in their efforts to escape from slavery. Snorton provides a detailed account of the escape of Ellen and William Craft in this respect and reads Ellen's cross-gendered and cross-racial performance as an example of what he calls the fungible passing into fugitive.

If *The Aggressives* highlights the difference that race makes to the trajectory of gender transition, other studies have contextualized the relationship between trans people and medicine within global capitalism, transnational movement, and the politics of citizenship. Aren Aizura's book *Mobile Subjects: Travel, Transnationality, and Transgender Lives* (in progress), on the politics of mobility for transgender and transsexual subjects, mostly transgender women, within global capitalism, is a case in point, blending careful textual analyses with original qualitative research on transsexuals seeking sex reassignment surgeries in Thailand and elsewhere.[19] The book also contains informative and clear accounts of the shifting meanings of gender variance and inspired theoretical conjecture about flexibility, mobility, and processes of subjectification. Aizura, like Latham, tries to hold open the meaning of trans\* experience in order to tell many stories at once about transgender bodies. Aizura concludes his book with a look at ethnographic research on gender reassignment surgeries for transwomen in a number of locales, most notably Bangkok. Such studies remind us of how often transgender theory uncritically produces a global narrative of gender and transformation that builds around the figure of a white, first-world migrant subject. Aizura unpacks the politics of location, the "grammars of mobility," and the "patterns of movement" within which all trans-gender processes are embedded. He also moves smoothly back and forth between social theory and careful attention to the mate-riality of transgender women's experience.

While work by Dean Spade and Toby Beauchamp orient more to the law and social sciences,[20] Aizura, like Latham, uses his own gender reassignment surgeries as a jumping-off point and applies his theoretical models to a series of case studies of surgi-cal tourism. These cases mostly involve first-world transsexual women visiting Thailand for sex reassignment surgery, and they allow Aizura to switch from thinking about transgender people as global consumers to situating the movements of transgender health care givers in a global marketplace of service labor. Aizura thus never gives in to the temptation to render transgender sub-jects only as a kind of subaltern; he recognizes precisely how transgender women can circulate both as bearers of a hegemonic order and as migrant workers in a global workplace.

The work I have considered in this chapter charts the uneven and unpredictable ways in which trans* bodies are inhabited, expe-rienced, constructed, deconstructed, read, rejected, embraced, and classified. The U.S. focus of this book contributes in some ways to the hegemonic depiction of transgenderism as a Euro-American phenomenon and as a creation of a liberal democracy within which everyone is supposedly encouraged to "be themselves." This is of course a deeply misleading frame within which to assess the privilege and the jeopardy of being trans* in North America, for it centers on the experiences of affluent, white transsexuals with access to health care and multiple sources of support. Such narra-tives serve as convenient fictions for the ongoing imperial project of centering North America in global narratives of progress, free-dom, and economic aspiration. The reality of the experience of becoming trans* in the United States is quite different depending on one's location, one's race and class background, and one's access to health care, and of course all of these factors play out differently for transgender women than for transgender men. But the narrative of the expansiveness of the U.S. system is bolstered by a tendency to project transphobic and homophobic regimes onto other countries.

In an independent film released in Germany in 2005, *Unveiled,* director Angelina Maccarone offers a damning critique of neo-colonial fantasies of intolerant others in the Middle East. The film plots the landscape of global exchange within which Muslim countries serve as intolerant foils against which the benevolence of Western liberal tolerance can be emphasized. Its original German title was *Fremde Haut* (literally, "foreign skin" or "stranger's skin"), the UN term for asylum seekers. As the Wikipedia article about the film explains, asylum seekers are spoken about as "fremde Haut" or "in orbit" "because they can actually find legal domicile nowhere at all."²¹

The film is about an Iranian woman who leaves Iran and her female lover for fear of legal punishment, then passes as a male as she seeks asylum in Germany; as such, it addresses a complex host of issues about gender, sexuality, migration, labor, exile, language, culture, race, and location. The notion proffered by the original title of asylum seekers as "in orbit," as lost in space or in perpetual motion, frames the film quite differently than the English title, *Unveiled.* While the English title fits comfortably into hegemonic U.S. constructions of the closet and visibility, it also links the discourse on visibility to one of freedom by playing on Western anxieties about the meaning of various forms of head coverings for Muslim women. The German title, *Fremde Haut,* refuses both the easy logic of visible/invisible that is implied by the notion of veiling and the inside/outside logic that the idea of being in a "foreign skin" prefers; instead, it places the emphasis on motion, transition, flight, precariousness, and inbetweenness.

*Fremde Haut* tells the story of Fariba Tabrizi (Jasmin Tabatabai), a queer Iranian who fears that she will be jailed or worse if her relationship with another woman becomes public. Fariba arrives in Germany after a long plane ride and then stays in a refugee center with other asylum seekers, among them Siamak (Navid Akhaven), a young political activist. Siamak's application for asylum is granted, but he kills himself in despair over his family in Iran. Fariba's application is denied because "lesbianism" is not a valid excuse for leaving Iran. So when she finds Siamak's lifeless body, she makes a decision to take on his persona. After burying his body respectfully, she dresses as Siamak, takes his papers, and assumes the responsibility for writing to his family. As Siamak, Fariba finds work illegally in a cabbage factory and begins a romance with a German woman, Anna (Anneke Kim Surnau). In the developing relationship between Fariba/Siamak and Anna, the film manages to address not only the queerness of the relationship but also the trans*ness of the precarious life of the asylum seeker. Balanced as s/he is between nations, identities, and legibility, the asylum seeker traces a trans* orbit as s/he moves passes back and forth between legal and illegal, man and woman, citizen and foreigner. By naming this space inbetween as trans*, we begin to see the importance of mutual articulations of race, nation, migration, and sexuality.

In addressing sexual citizenship, queer Muslims, sexuality and religion, space/location and desire, the film draws our attention to the radically transformed European landscape of the late twentieth and early twenty-first centuries where we find new forms of queer activism and trans* identity. Scholar Fatima El-Tayeb, in her book *European Others,* has written at length on race and queerness in Europe and about persistent, anachronistic, and dangerous understandings of race in a European context. In a chapter titled "Secular Submissions: Muslim Europeans, Female Bodies, and Performative Politics," for example, El-Tayeb situates queer Muslim youth as the fantasized "outside" of Europe and swiftly exposes the interdependent and simultaneous construction of a Western commitment to rights alongside the production of a population who threaten those rights and therefore must be deprived of their own.[22]

These fantasies of a thoroughly antimodern, violent otherness embodied in Muslims play out in *Fremde Haut* in the figure of the transitive and transgendered subject who finds himself at the mercy of continued German investments in whiteness and white nationhood. As we see in the film, Fariba's decision to cross-dress and pass coincides with her desire to seek asylum—the fact that asylum depends literally on her being someone else implies the pressures to conform, assimilate, and integrate that attend to every effort to relocate for people moving from certain parts of the world to Europe.

In his oft-quoted work on refugee status and the "state of exception," *Homo Sacer,* Giorgio Agamben speaks of the contradiction whereby international human rights are said to be crafted for those "in orbit," asylum seekers, but they actually work by excluding such people from access to rights.[23] Agamben is interested in naming and putting into relation all those people who lie outside the representational capacities of the state, and he identifies Jews and Gypsies as examples. Here we could advocate for a queer alliance of the dispossessed and the precarious—the Jews and Gypsies in some historical moments, the

Asian migrant laborer in another, the Muslim activist in yet another, the diasporic queer in still another. The trans* embodiment that Fariba/Siamak represents in *Fremde Haut* is a reminder that identities and modes of embodiment shift in meaning and form as people cross boundaries and find themselves subject to new and different kinds of regulation. It would not be right to see this character as simply passing, as trans or as a man; by taking up the identity of his dead comrade, the trans* character fully embraces the necessity of improvising identity in a world in which the refugee falls between the cracks of power, representation, and protection.

I attended a screening of *Unveiled* at a London film festival shortly after its release, after which the lead actor, Jasmin Tabatabai, took questions from the audience. Most concerned the persecution of gays and lesbians in Iran. Tabatabai expressed confusion; the film, after all, was not about Iran per se, it was about the fantasy of sanctuary offered by European countries like Germany, a promise that turns out to be empty at best, a new site of danger and violence at worst. In the end, it was impossible to get a conversation going about the intersections of transphobia, homophobia, and anti-immigrant sentiment in Germany or about the film's use of a queer relationship to highlight the tension between the commonsense narratives of an expansive German immigration policy that offers solace to refugees from intolerant Muslim countries, on the one hand, and the harsh reality of new forms of German nationalism that define themselves over and against Muslim citizens, on the other.

Central to the plot of *Unveiled* is the contradiction within which Iranian lesbians are neither tolerated nor openly persecuted. Fariba could not gain asylum in Germany as a lesbian because Iran has no overt policy against lesbianism. This conundrum, in which an identity is neither sustainable nor grounds for establishing residency elsewhere, speaks to the complicated attitudes toward trans* subjects outside of Euro-American contexts. In Iran, homosexuality is not exactly prohibited, and the state actually supports sex reassignment surgeries for transsexuals. The emergence of state-sponsored support for sex reassignment and transgender health care in Iran, however, has been cast as part of a theocratic, indeed Islamic, attempt to convert "deviant homosexuals" into normative men and women. That said, Afsaneh Najmabadi, in her 2013 book *Professing Selves: Transsexuality and Same-Sex Desire in Contemporary Iran,* offers a counternarrative to this explanation for Iranian support of transsexual medical care. In a meticulously researched account of the biomedical management of transsexuality in Iran, Najmabadi argues that while the original impetus for state intervention may well have come from a context in which "sex change is framed explicitly as the cure for a diseased abnormality," that is not the end of the story.[24] Just because the state offers sex reassignment surgery as a transit route from aberration to normality, that does not mean this is always how the medical intervention will be used. Indeed, Najmabadi finds that very often the mechanisms used by the Iranian state to assess and filter sex and gender "deviants" into treatment end up generating "a porously marked, nebulous, and spacious domain populated by a variety of 'not-normal' people."[25]

In other words, state-sponsored projects, even deeply conservative ones with the explicit intention of converting gender-variant people into normal men and women, have unpredictable effects and may well enable the emergence of broad coalitions of "not-normal people." By the same token, in the context of seemingly liberal contexts like the United States, trans* people can find themselves without any support, and sometimes they are forced to converse with conservative and religious groups to get assistance. For very precarious trans* women in particular, for whom work is hard to come by and sex work is often the default, a state-sponsored project offering hormones and surgery would be more than welcome.

These alternative representations of trans* lives, like *Unveiled,* map a global frame for considering the production of trans* embodiment. All too often within an imperial frame produced and sustained in North American contexts, transgender bodies might be cast as evidence of primitive or premodern modes of existence (as in anthropological accounts of Indigenous trans* subjects); as part of a state-sponsored attempt to eliminate gay and lesbian lifestyles (as in Iran); as mobile consumers of medical tourism (as in Thailand); or as first-world beneficiaries of U.S. benevolence and technological advancement. None of these constructions of trans* lives are "true," and none are simply false. All, however, can be placed alongside the record of the fabulous, inventive, dis-identificatory processes by which and through which trans* people dream themselves into the world and remake the world in the process.

THREE

# Becoming Trans*

ELISABETH: Your parents want what's best for you.
LUDO: They don't know what's best for me.
*Ma Vie en Rose*, dir. Alain Berliner (1997)

When I was a young ... person ... I was constantly taken for a boy, and my parents were frantic to intervene in the relentless gendering of me as male. I was forced to wear my hair long and dress in girlish clothing, and told to sit and stand a certain way. The embarrassment of my gender often involved a wide cast of characters—I stood at the center of a theatrical production playing out daily around my queerness and within an ever more complicated staging of the child body. A stranger/distant relative/shopkeeper would say, "What a wonderful family, two girls, two boys!" and beam with contentment at the symmetry thus observed. But of course, the symmetry was of their own making. "Three girls and a boy," my father would interject. Pause. Cue me—and now I had to perform in a girlish way to throw off the cover of maleness that I had so happily assumed. Pause. Well, lovely family. End of conversation.

The break in symmetry performed by my emergence as "girl" from the cover of "boy" that I had eagerly worn and inhabited was in actual fact a much larger rupture and one that not only undermines the supposed "loveliness" of the family but also one that comes, in the larger culture, to stand for the problem with family per se. Family names a system that is supposed to protect, enclose, and embrace its members, but, like any system of membership, it as often excludes, shames, and savages outsiders. The presence of cross-gendered children and gender-ambiguous children within the family throws all kinds of assumptions about gender, childhood, and embodiment into question and ultimately casts doubt on the validity of the family itself.

In 2015, after functioning for at least half a century as the name for bodily disgrace and gender absurdity, "transgender" (used as an umbrella term for gender-variant bodies) became a household word. What with debates about bathroom use and regular appearances of transgender people on TV shows and within celebrity culture, the term suddenly circulated widely, and it came to the point where not a day went by without some kind of news story on transgender people in bathrooms, in the military, in the law, in sports, in school, in fact and fiction and everything in between. Transgender thus became and remains the newest marker of exclusion and pathology to be seamlessly transitioned into a template for acceptance and tolerance. While we should undoubtedly celebrate recent attention to transgender rights, transgender visibility, and transgender recognition—not to mention trans\* access to public facilities—we must also resist some of the streamlining effects of this recognition and ask what price will be paid and by whom for this new visibility. Much of the new conversation about gender focuses on children's bodies and gender identities and seeks to remedy social exclusion on their behalf. Indeed, the emergence of trans* children in families around the United States may well be the foundation for this new national conversation. Of course, within such conversations about gender justice the trans* child in question is typically white, and the sense of wanting to protect the child and usher her/him into the gendered adolescence s/he desires does not extend to children living in poverty, many children of color, and trans* youth who are delivered into the juvenile justice system, often through what has been called the "school–to-prison pipeline."

Trans activism has often been folded into the lesbian and gay rights movements that began in the 1970s and culminated in the removal of lesbianism and gay identity from various medical definitions of pathology. But as lesbians and gay men earned recognition and protection from the state, transgender people often came to occupy the newly vacated classifications of disorder and dysfunction. And so, while the American Psychiatric Association removed homosexuality from its *Diagnostic and Statistical Manual of Mental Disorders (DSM)* in the early 1970s, "gender identity disorder" remained listed until as recently as 2013.[1] Its eventual removal is not all-good news, however; although cross-gender identification has been cleared of the stigma of a disorder, attention has now shifted to what is called "gender dysphoria." Someone suffering from "gender dysphoria," according to the most recent (fifth) edition of *DSM,* exhibits distress over their gendered embodiment and may require treatment. As with past definitions of LGT identities, there is no accounting here for the fact that a person's distress over their gender identity may be the result of social exclusion, family violence, or reduced employment opportunities rather than of a struggle with gender identification.

Because transsexuality and transgenderism have different definitional trajectories than lesbian or gay identifications, transgender activism has been understood, in the last few decades, as a separate and fairly discrete category of political organizing with its own relations to respectability, on the one hand, and rebellion on the other. National organizations such as the National Center for Transgender Equality (NCTE) is, according to its mission statement, "a national social justice organization devoted to ending discrimination and violence against transgender people through education and advocacy on national issues of importance to transgender people."[2] Like lesbian and gay national organizations, NCTE uses the language of empowerment as well as the channels of mainstream political lobbying and has a stated goal of equality. NCTE also pursues employment opportunities, legal protection, and health care access for transgender people, as well as access to accurate identity documentation. But this kind of organizing does not seek to challenge or change any of the underlying social conditions that lead to the acceptance of some transgender people into public life and the criminalization and marginalization of other "less deserving" gender-variant folks.

At the other end of the spectrum we can look at groups such as the Sylvia Rivera Law Project (SLRP), a radical nonprofit organization advocating for the freedom of all people to "self-determine their gender identity and expression, regardless of income or race, and without facing harassment, discrimination, or violence."[3] The SLRP advocates for transgender youth, homeless people, immigrants, and prisoners; its efforts reveal the massive disparities in the life experiences of young and poor transgender people versus those of wealthy, often white transgender professionals. Dean Spade, one of the founders of SLRP, articulates the differences among transgender people in terms of reduced or enhanced life chances, cautioning that "the most marginalized trans people experience more extreme vulnerability, in part because more aspects of their lives are directly controlled by legal and administrative systems of domination—prisons, welfare programs, foster care, drug treatment centers, homeless shelters, job training centers—that employ rigid gender binaries. These intersecting vectors of control make obtaining resources especially difficult, restrict access to zones of retreat or safety, and render every loss of a job, family support, or access to an advocate or a health care opportunity more costly."[4]

Spade replaces a generalized understanding of discrimination based on superficial markers of difference, such as skin color, with a more structural model pointing to the greater vulnerability of poor people and people of color due to the "legal and administrative systems of domination." For transgender people, this domination intensifies to the extent that they must petition for hormones, surgery, employment protection, name change, and so on, and if they cannot afford to do so, they become illegible and therefore dangerous within the systems charged with surveying, managing, and controlling those populations with the least to gain from the status quo. These differentials in vulnerability to violence and poverty are a crucial part of understanding how transgender people are welcomed and recognized by some laws and controlled and confined by others.

By this logic, we could say that in the first two decades of the twenty-first century transgender bodies have come to represent new frontiers for state recognition, social tolerance, and flexible norms. The warm embrace of the state, the family, the school, and the military is now extended to the very bodies that previously signified the abject limits to belonging. But these new modes of acceptance extended only to forms of transgender embodiment that could be easily identified with new markets for capital. They did not extend to categories of transgender life that remain challenging to a politics of respectability, legality, and legibility. In this way, the new icons of transgender life include Caitlin Jenner, a wealthy former athlete and a part of the Kardashian media empire; Laverne Cox, a Black transgender woman who plays a transgender prisoner in *Orange Is the New Black;* and numerous transgender children who have challenged bathroom restrictions in their schools. This iconography has not, however, extended to transgender sex workers or transgender victims of sexual violence, homeless transgender youth or transgender people of color living in neighborhoods subject to police brutality and cast as gang zones by state officials.

If "queer" in the 1990s and 2000s was the marker of a politics of sex and gender that exceeded identity and gestured toward a critique of state power and assimilationist goals, we could say the term "trans*" marks a politics based on a general instability of identity and oriented toward social transformation, not political accommodation. As the term "transgender" comes to represent the acceptable edge of gender variance, the category of trans* signifies the cost of that level of acceptance. The category takes the prefix for transitivity and couples it with the asterisk that indicates a wildcard in internet searches; it is a diacritical mark that poses a question to its prefix and stands in for what exceeds the politics of naming and recognition. Trans* also signals the insufficiency of current classificatory systems, many of which we inherited from the nineteenth and early twentieth centuries. The solution, as I discussed earlier, is not to impose ever more precise calibrations of bodily identity but rather to think in new and different ways about what it means to claim a body.

In terms of gendered embodiment, as the work of so many queer scholars on race and sexuality shows, contemporary definitions of femininity and masculinity, as well as current formulations of gender fluidity, lean heavily on concepts of the gendered body adapted from early twentieth-century formulations of race and class. For example, while historian Gail Bederman in *Manliness and Civilization* is very persuasive about the catastrophic consequences in the early twentieth century of battles fought by white men against Black male bodies on behalf of what they felt was a destabilized and crumbling social order,[5] more recently Black queer scholars have investigated the foundations of white femininity with its reliance on the criminalization of Black women. Sarah Haley, for example, in a stunning account of state violence directed at young Black women at the start of the twentieth century in the United States, discovers that "imprisoned black women were labeled queer in the years immediately preceding the word being used to describe homosexual desire and homosexuals." This leads her to the startling insight that "the imprisoned black female subject was, in some ways, vestibular to queerness." Using the sense of the "vestibular" that Hortense Spillers pioneered in her essay on Black (un)gendering, "Mama's Baby, Papa's Maybe," Haley draws attention to the ways in which "black women became a point of passage between what was normative and what was queer."[6] The queerness that the legal system ascribed to Black bodies disqualified those same bodies from any protection against injustice and indeed made them available for intense brutality at the hands of the law.

The fact that current definitions and uses of the term "queer" proceed without a clear sense of the centrality of bodies of color to the production of its meaning suggests that one function of sex/gender classifications is the occlusion of the operations of white supremacy within seemingly natural systems of naming. The term "trans*" uses the asterisk to hold open the many histories of variant bodies and the many ways in which those histories have been deployed.

And while the nonspecificity of the term might be considered its strength, some transgender commentators have critiqued "trans*" precisely because of its bagginess and lack of specificity. Still others, however, like Eva Haywood and Jami Weinstein in a great essay titled "Tranimalities," have celebrated the asterisk for its ranginess and have taken the term to the very limit of the human:

> The asterisk, a diminutive astral symbol miming a starfish's limby reach, follows trans and attaches to it, attaches it to something else, a spiky allergenic pollen soliciting immunological mobilizations, a viral latching-on to membraneous surfaces of words. Trans* is meant, in part, to break open the category of transgender, transwoman, or transman. It is recognized as "an effort" (after all, an asterisk can suggest emphasis, which is perhaps also affective) to include all noncisgender identities. The * is a paratactic: it denotes a database search, it designates multiplication, it can be a disclaimer indexing the fine print, it indicates pseudonyms or names that have been changed, and, in computer code, asterisks around a word will embolden it. The multi-pointed asterisk is fingery; it both points and touches.[7]

This great riff on the asterisk pays attention not only to the symbol's diacritical function but also to its form—its star shape—its indexical or haptic function. Recognizing in its shape the "starfish's limby reach" (a research interest of Hayward's), Hayward and Weinstein connect the linguistic sign to a different kind of body with a different relation to signification, symbolization, metaphor, and emphasis. My use of the asterisk, like theirs, embraces the nonspecificity of the term "trans" and uses it to open the term up to a shifting set of conditions and possibilities rather than to attach it only to the life narratives of a specific group of people. Gender variance, we might say, is both the history of difference and the history of how difference has been deployed within a commitment to the status quo. Having stressed the differences between various trans* subject positions in the context of a U.S. political system that guarantees protection and rights to some only by denying these to others, let us try to parse acceptable and unacceptable forms of being by focusing briefly on the figure of the white and middle-class transgender child and the attention such children have received within the latest political battles around bathroom use, gender pronouns, and the recognition of people's chosen gender identities. In contrast to transgender activism over the past fifty years, which has sought transformative ways around binary definitions and the systems of control that such binaries impose and uphold, new activism on behalf of often very young children by their parents seeks mostly to normalize the child and keep radicalization at bay. This new wave of neoliberal incorporation seeks to situate the transgender person, and often the transgender child specifically, as a victim in need of protection, a minor in need of advocacy, or a patient in need of care. The discourses, medical and psychological and otherwise, that attend to the trans* child sit uneasily alongside a new suite of narratives about disability and accommodations for all kinds of forms of debilitating differences.

Whereas even a few decades ago transsexuality was considered a "condition" that was typically expressed and addressed only in early adulthood, currently children as young as four years old may express various forms of gender variance, and there are now protocols for parents and teachers who have concerns about the gender-questioning children in their care. These parents and teachers, well-meaning though they are, might be accused of organizing from above, in the sense that they attempt to intuit what their very young children need as they express varying degrees of gender ambiguity and they try to mold education and medicine to those needs rather than surrendering their children to the needs of the community at large. These are noble goals and they coincide with some of the trajectories that families of intersex children fought for a decade or so ago. But they still put in place an activism that works around rather than through the child, and in so doing this activism has prematurely stabilized the meaning of the trans* child's gender variance and put protocols in place for the normalization of his or her gender.

Nowadays, it is the parents of gender-variant children for the most part who have initiated fights about the use of bathrooms in schools. While parents are insisting on the rights of their children to use the restroom that is most comfortable for them, we might want to ask bigger questions about restroom designations in general and the various gendered and racial restrictions to which they have historically been subject. The issue here is not simply about insisting that trans* children use a specific bathroom but about granting all children access to all restrooms. Some schools are trying to work around legislating restroom usage one child at a time by eliminating urinals in favor of single-stall toilets that any child can access. This is approach recognizes that a shift has occurred in the culture that requires whole-scale solutions, not piecemeal workarounds that continue to center on the "problem" of the gender-variant body.

Children may well represent the front lines of change in gender protocols. If the child absorbs the wisdom of their era, then surely the three- or four-year-old who declares themself to be definitively a gender at odds with their birth-assigned sex is a harbinger of a new world of embodiment. But by the same token, might the emergence of the transgender child in white middle-

class households actually signal new articulations of family structures: what the family once formally excluded and denounced
(gender and sexual "deviants"), it now includes and claims? What
is the significance of the emergence of transgender children?

The instability of childhood means that gender is necessarily
uncertain before heteronormative family dynamics shape it into
something clear and "true." The child can therefore be a vehicle
for both the most normative of social fantasies and the most flam-
boyant of social fears. Indeed, in the past the child has been
feared as a channel for social denouncement (think of the child in
*The Children's Hour* who informs on her "lesbian" teachers); as a
recipient of ideological brainwashing (think of Ariel Dorfman's
*How to Read Donald Duck,* a book about the imperial function of
Disney cartoons); an enforcer of socially repugnant rules that the
child may not even understand (Nazi youth, for example). The
child has also figured as the site for the staging of potent alterna-
tives, as an unruly agent that must be tamed, as a block to business as usual and an anarchistic site of refusal (think of Max from
*Where the Wild Things Are*). Children, in other words, are dense
figures of social anxiety and aspiration both. For this reason, the
way that discourses on gender and sexuality circulate through
them gives us much information about how normalization works.

In relation to the emergence of trans-variable bodies, accordingly, the trans* child, or the child uncertain of their gender orientation, represents a gender instability that the family has both
cultivated and rejected. In contemporary contexts, "the transgender child," a clearly identified and identifiable subject, has
been offered up as a resolution to childhood issues with gender
variance. The transgender child is a product of social media, the
object of new and public conversations about gender instability,
the subject of several generations of activism—and now they

have become the cause célèbre of new modes of parental activism. As such, the transgender child raises questions about whether new modes of gendered embodiment pose any challenge at all to cultural and social norms.

In the past, trans* children have been represented in film and media not as victims in need of assistance and advocacy but as trespassers in the family home, as flies in the ointment, as disturbed and disturbing. In *Ma Vie en Rose* (1997, dir. Alain Berliner), for example, a brightly colored childhood arranges itself around an adorable femme boy who prefers long hair and flowery clothes to short hair and sports. He is delightful and beloved, kind and unique, but the community within which his family is embedded makes him and his family aware of the fact that his blatant femininity is not to be tolerated. The blame for his overt expressions of femininity is cast on his mother, for being too sexy; his father, for not being authoritarian; his grandmother, for not being married; and finally, on the boy himself, for being "weak." *Ma Vie en Rose*, remarkably, while it does present its young trans*-hero as at odds with their community in suburban Belgium, manages to present viewers with a sense of the resilience of the trans* child and his/her wayward desires. Ludo never calls himself a transgender child; he simply occupies a space of experimentation.

And in Céline Sciamma's beautiful drama from 2011 titled *Tomboy*, ten-year-old Laure struggles when her family moves to a new neighborhood. This moment of geographical transition places the child and her younger sister in the precarious social milieu faced by "new kids" everywhere, but in the case of Laure, a cute and boyish child, it affords an opportunity as well to present herself according to her own desires rather than those of her parents and family. When the new kids that Laure encounters and plays football with presume Laure is male, he goes along with it and calls himself Mikael, despite having a prepubescent female body. Mikael is clearly relieved and energized by the freedom and recognition that his new identity brings and he revels in his status among the boys and the attention he draws from girls, especially one girl with whom he begins a romantic interaction. As the movie plays out, there are lows and highs, love and disappointment, and finally, as in so many of these films, revelation/discovery/exposure and, ultimately, punishment.

Despite the unhappy ending to *Tomboy*, this film, along with *Ma Vie en Rose*, brings into dramatic relief a few fundamental facts about bourgeois notions of childhood and gender as they have played out in the past through the unwelcome spectacle of the trans* child:

1. *Children see the world differently than adults do.*
   *Tomboy*'s opening clip dramatizes this insight. We see an
   image of a child drawing a child, and while we recognize
   in the flat stick figure a kind of universal representation of
   childhood drawing skills, we also are asked to think about
   the image not just as "rudimentary" but as evidence of a
   fundamentally different worldview. Whereas adults tend
   to "see" gender in normative ways, children can be
   content with appearances and do not always believe in
   deep, essential structures that layer the self in contradictory and uneven ways until taught to do so by adults. This
   image of a child representing a child reminds us that the
   condition of childhood is the condition of *being represented
   by adults*—children have little control over the mode of
   representation but are constantly subject to it. *Tomboy* and
   *Ma Vie en Rose* ask us to consider and remember what the
   world looks like from a child's-eye view. It also makes a

visual case for seeing the world through child eyes: as candy colored and full of wonder, in the case of Ludo in *Ma Vie en Rose*, and as vibrant and pulsating with erotic promise, in the case of Mikael in *Tomboy*. But it reminds us as well that childhood is a time of brutality, cruelty, and violence, and while the other children accept Ludo and Mikael as long as they do not disturb the balance of power in the fragile networks between children and adults, they turn on them once the adults become enraged.

2. *Gender is attributed as much as it is declared.*

In *Tomboy*, Mikael's gender is a collaborative event that occurs among and between the children. He presents as male despite living with a female body; they accept his child body as male whether or not they believe it. Only when the adults have declared a mismatch do they demand proof. Gender always comes from elsewhere rather than forming the truth of the body. This is a concept that was beautifully laid out back in 1978 by sociologists Wendy McKenna and Suzanne Kessler in their groundbreaking book *Gender: An Ethnomethodological Approach*.[8] There, the authors both describe and explain the centrality of gender attribution to the production of systems of gender recognition and identity. By gender attribution, they mean the ways in which we all ascribe genders to all the bodies we encounter by rapidly scanning bodies and making assumptions about their morphologies and orientations. Kessler and McKenna also note, far ahead of poststructuralist gender theory, that biology is not the key to gender attribution. Instead of gender attribution, a split-second assessment, being based on genitalia, they note, genitalia are mostly *assumed*. With these arguments, they laid the foundations for Judith Butler's famous formulation in *Gender Trouble:* that gender does not emerge as a cultural interpretation of sex, but rather, sex circulates as a cultural interpretation of gender.[9]

While McKenna and Kessler's theories of gender attribution and Butler's theories of gender performativity have had enormous staying power over the last twenty years, they have also been contested by transgender activists for whom the body or the materiality of gender has a kind of stubborn persistence. And as we shall see, many transgender theorists have produced radically different accounts of gendered subjectivity, accounts that insist on rather than attempt to sidestep the flesh, its meaning, and its plasticity or fixity.

3. *The child is a screen onto whom gender normativity is projected but who reminds us of the variation that is spontaneous within presocial subjects.*

Normativity, we know from Michel Foucault, is a central part of modern power systems, and it works by disciplining complex societies through self-policing mechanisms. In his *History of Sexuality,* Foucault, using the example of the "masturbating child," sees the child body as a place where social expectations are enforced over and against, through and within, whatever expressions of identity and desire may emerge in the oversurveyed and multiply interpreted terrain of childhood.[10]

Ultimately, a child body can slip through the matrix of parental and pedagogical supervision, but a system of normativity works both through the exertion of pressure against nonnormative behavior and through the internalization of standards of conduct that are communicated silently and even gesturally. Children of all backgrounds, in other words, are supposed to internalize models of gender and reproduce them in forms that match up with their cultural, racial, and classed locations and in relation to manners, gender-appropriate likes and dislikes, conventional interactions within a heterosexual matrix, and even their own hopes and fears about the future.

New modes of parenting among white middle-class "designer" parents have shifted the coordinates of belonging such that the trans* child that might previously have been viewed as disruptive might now be displayed as a trophy, a mark of the family's flexibility, a sign of the liberal family's capacious borders. The trans* child is also placed by their parents within an ever-expanding and dizzying array of disabilities that the parents claim for their children and then seek to cure, ameliorate, or medicalize. Jasbir Puar, in an extraordinary essay on the overlap between discourses of disability and models of transgenderism, comments on the sometimes contradictory and sometimes complementary goals of transgender and disability activism. Puar explains how transgenderism has been excluded from the category of disability both to purge disability of any connection to perverse gendering but also to protect transgenderism from pathologization. In the process, however, both discourses reinvest in normativity and create narratives that "suffer from a domination of whiteness and contend with normativization of the acceptable and recognizable subject."[11] Using a framework of capacity and debility to mark the shuttling of bodies between productivity and neediness, Puar helpfully shows how, within capitalism, normalization revalues bodies that have otherwise been reviled and rejected while making distinctions between differently located trans and disabled bodies. It is this process that transforms the gender-variant child from an abject and potentially unlovable body into an exceptional sign of uniqueness that reflects value back onto the family and heteronormative systems of care, and diverts attention away from other genealogies of becoming. For Puar, ultimately, we must resist discourses that posit an end point to transitions or a cure for disabilities in favor of a notion of "becoming trans" which highlights "the impossibility of linearity, permanence, and end points."[12] Such a model refuses the exceptionality of the transgender subject, allows for various relations to biopolitical power and access, and, ultimately, forecloses on the transgender child as a foundation for a transgender adult future.

Ultimately, then, *Tomboy* and *Ma Vie en Rose* make us aware of how forcefully parents "train" children to be "normal," how blatantly adults insist on certain forms of embodiment and forbid others. In fact, there is nothing natural in the end about gender as it emerges from childhood; the hetero scripts that are forced on children have nothing to do with nature and everything to do with violent enforcements of hetero-reproductive domesticity. These enforcements, even when they can accommodate some degree of bodily difference, direct children toward regular understandings of the body in time and space. But the weird set of experiences that we call childhood stands outside adult logics of time and space. The time of the child, then, like the time of the queer, is always already over and still to come. As Kathryn Bond Stockton puts it, "The child is precisely who we are not and, in fact, never were. It is the act of the adults looking back."[13] Childhood, for Stockton, is ghostly: it haunts adulthood, eludes children, and becomes a misty presence and a palpable absence all at once. Childhood is over in the sense that we theorize it retrospectively from the vantage point of normative adulthood in the context of modernity, and it is still to come in the sense that normative adulthood is only held in place by the relegation of all forms of otherness to the past. Childhood in the past was never queer, never trans*, always oriented toward a normativity to come. The arrival of trans* children disrupts not only the meaning of the gendered body but our understandings of time, development, and order itself.

# FOUR

# Trans* Generations

A house—they are families for a lot of people
who don't have families; but this is a new meaning
of family.

> Dorian Corey, in *Paris Is Burning,*
> dir. Jennie Livingston (1990)


Trans* people of a certain age can typically recall the moment they first saw an ambiguously gendered person. For me, as for many of my generation, it was my gym teacher. She was an impressively muscular woman who stood, ran, and threw "like a man." Ms. S——, as we had to call her, wore a tracksuit every day: usually it was a red stretch nylon suit with jaunty white stripes down the sides of the jacket and the pants. Ms. S—— barked orders like an army drill sergeant, and she taught us how to hit a hockey ball long and far and how to muscle others out of the play. Even as I recognized something familiar in Ms. S——, she too recognized something queer about me and singled me out for extra coaching. Later, I met drag queens and the occasional drag king in New York City in the 1980s, and I always wondered if it was really possible to live a life in a body that was not fully legible as either male or female. A few butch academics—Esther Newton in particular—allowed me to imagine myself as a professional without femming up, and in time, I'm sure, I probably modeled a certain credible form of alternative masculinity for others as well.

Cross-generational contact has been crucial for trans* people over the past four or five decades, making it possible for young people to imagine themselves as trans* adults. In the past two decades, however, such contact has been replaced with a kind of rivalry, an oedipal tension if you like, and young trans* people increasingly discover information about themselves online rather than through older trans* people. In a context where many transgender kids pass through queer youth groups, queer and trans* adults can sometimes be cast as the enemy. In worst-case scenarios, older generations are seen as potential predators in relation to trans* and queer youth and viewed with suspicion. It seems now, in some ways, as if older and younger trans* people occupy different realities and think differently about the past and future. This chapter attempts to address, and hopefully bridge, this growing gap.

In the opening minutes of Jennie Livingston's 1990 documentary *Paris Is Burning*, Pepper Labeija introduces themself: "I am Pepper Labeija, legendary mother of the House of Labeija." As the film unfolds, it tells a layered story of the queer ball scene of New York City in the 1980s. This scene, where people of color in drag perform, dance, and vogue their way to a certain degree of subcultural fame, brims with makeshift and brilliantly improvised relationships to glamour, work, realness, and family. In this opening interview, Pepper Labeija identifies as the "mother" of her house and notes the importance of her position in a world where young people of color are scrambling to survive. Her words are echoed later by grand dame Dorian Corey, who offers pithy formulations of queer and trans* life. Corey comments on the existence of houses such as Labeija's, saying: "A house—they are families for a lot of people who don't have families; but this is a new meaning of family. The hippies had families, and no one thought nothing about it. It wasn't a question of a man, a woman, and children, which we grew up knowing as family; it is a question of a group of human beings in a mutual bond."[1] This remade understanding of family, kinship, and cross-generational care in the context of drag houses was one of the most important legacies of the film and offers still an enduring reminder that mainstream notions of family have little to do with many of the ways in which queer and trans* people of color have created life under harsh conditions, one expressive of their "mutual bond."

*Paris Is Burning* has been critiqued over the years, but it remains an important record of a subcultural world at a particular point in time. One of its most important contributions concerns the alternative forms of kinship created by the drag queens, mothers, fathers, and children in this mostly Black and Latino performance universe. The film also provides a fairly extensive visual account of trans* life in the 1980s, well before transgender identities were part of the national conversation. While Livingston's film functions today mainly as archival footage of an early moment in trans* history, the ball culture itself continues. In his book *Butch Queens Up in Pumps,* a fuller account of the ball scene past and present, Marlon Bailey provides a more elaborate set of understandings of cross-generational trans* care and trans* performance cultures.[2] The book reimagines kinship itself by tracing the complex sets of relations between the children of the houses, between the children and the parents, between the parents, between houses, between rival houses, and so on.

In his analysis of intergenerational relations, Bailey builds on the work of Chandan Reddy to explain the complexity of both gender and family in this subculture. Reddy, in an essay titled "Houses, Homes, Non-Identity," uses the house system to illustrate the ways in which capitalism and democracy often conflict, in the sense that while democracy articulates a theory of abstract equality, capitalism relies on hierarchies.[3] While Reddy's article, one of the best on the economy of the ball scene and its house system, wants to show how well the queens understand their relationship to wealth, home, and property within the uneven distribution of wealth in the United States, Bailey draws out the intricacies of the kinship system itself. Indeed, Bailey builds on a long tradition of queer anthropology, by Esther Newton, Kath Weston, and others, that reexamines the Lévi-Straussian concept of kinship in terms of chosen families and a critique of heteronorms.[4] Bailey writes: "Through houses, Ballroom members challenge conventional notions of marriage, family, and kinship by revising gender relations and redefining gendered labor within the kin unit. Primarily, the house is a social configuration, the principle through which the kin unit is organized. Yet, the house can also be a space where the members congregate, and it can be a literal home for Ballroom members."[5] Houses, in other words, recreate the actual networks of care upon which conventional families have reneged. They unite their members through performance practices, shared experiences of hardship, and a joyful interaction with forms of glamour and fame that otherwise seem out of reach. Far from false consciousness, the investment in fame that the children articulate, and that they inherit from their house mothers and fathers, actually recognizes the looping mechanisms of appropriation by which high fashion, modeling, superstardom, and dance derive inspiration from these subcultural worlds rather than vice versa. The account of queer and trans* kinship offered by both Bailey and Reddy is important in an era where the trans* child is mostly represented as a white and middle-class victim of pernicious gender ideologies that prevent her or him from dressing the way s/he wants, using the restroom s/he feels is most appropriate, and expressing a unique gender. The unique formulations of children and parents and houses in the ball scene emphasize how often we center white children's experiences when talking about "the child" and how central children have become to contemporary narratives of freedom and tolerance. This does not explain, however, how trans* children became so central in the early twenty-first century to emerging narratives of the U.S. family.

In a succinct entry for the keyword "The Child" in the first issue of the *Transgender Studies Quarterly,* sociologist Tey Meadow narrates the emergence of the transgender child: "A relatively new social form, we see no references to transgender children prior to the mid-1990s."⁶ Meadow continues in this keyword entry to provide a quick history of the category of trans-childhood and points to activism by parents on behalf of their gender-variant children in the early twenty-first century as key to the production of definitions and explanations for what gender-variant expression in very young children might mean. Meadow's account, powerful as it is, does not situate these gender-variant children alongside any other historical definitions of queer kinship.

Prior to the 1990s, a middle-class child who expressed a strong and abiding desire to be recognized as "the other sex" might have been described as having a gender identity disorder and perhaps even treated for psychological disturbances. Such a child might also have been understood as gay or lesbian and been a source of confusion and consternation for his or her parents. Presently, however, as Meadow's work chronicles, the gender-variant child has been the occasion for activism and outreach by parents and family members who seek not to restrain and reorient their gender-queer children but who advocate for them and recognize them in their gender-nonconforming identities. As Meadow's work also shows, intriguingly, this new generation of gender-variant children may experience their gender identity in vastly different ways vis-à-vis people just a decade older than them. Meadow describes this disjunction in transgender histories as follows: "Trans adults must cope with the deeply different trajectories and life chances of the smallest gender outlaws. Some of these children may elect to be stealth (maintain total privacy about their gender histories) as adults; some may never identify openly as transgender; many will never go through their natal puberties or retain childhood memory books filled with pictures that do not mirror their gender identities as adults. For these reasons, *this new generation may have wider latitude to disidentify with transgender history and with those who came before them*" (my italics).[7]

While Meadow does not follow up on this point in his short essay, it is a mind-blowing statement. Unlike in other social justice contexts where young people might acknowledge and even thank the adults who came before them and made the world a more hospitable place, Meadow proposes that the support that many white middle-class trans children now enjoy from their families and communities affords them a radically different experience of childhood than that of trans people even a decade older. While transgender individuals of my generation, now in their forties and fifties, often could not transition until they were adults, lacked a complex language for their gender variance, and had to live large parts of their lives conforming to gender identities with which they were at odds, today's gender-nonconforming children, with parental support, may grow up trans rather than struggling through long periods of enforced gender normativity. While that is cause for some amount of celebration, it also, Meadow suggests, puts these young people at odds with the history that produced the conditions for their smoother passage from trans childhood to adulthood.

And indeed, perhaps the disidentification that Meadow describes between a new generation of trans children/young adults and those that came before them is precisely what has given rise to the battles over naming that I summarized in the introduction. While for an older generation a term like "tranny" harkens back to a time when medical terminology dominated the landscape and forced gender-variant people to present in gender-normative bodies for long periods of their lives, for younger trans people the term speaks to a shadowy world where insults had to be rehabilitated and turned into identity claims and where "trans" was a marker of some kind of irresolvable damage and dysphoria. Indeed, "dysphoria" itself, a term that allowed earlier generations to explain their bodily discomfort, has fallen out of favor and stands as a reminder of the bad old days.

The open question of variability and its meanings is particularly meaningful when it comes to child and adolescent bodies. Again, Meadow reminds us that adult observations on children's gender identities are skewed by certain assumptions: "A central paradox animates all of these efforts to define the transgender child. While most adults understand gender development teleologically, they still struggle with whether and how to distinguish childhood self-knowledge from adult identity. They labor to determine if gender is ever fluid or stable, unfinished or finished, a property of the self or a creation of the outside world."[8] In other words, for some children, their gender variance is the beginning of a lifelong sense of gender nonconformity. For others, gender variance is a stage to pass through; and for still others gender variance in childhood has little or no connection to how they might identify as adults. For example, some children have a sense of being in the "wrong body" that is so pronounced that they cannot function until their sense of their gender variance is acknowledged and addressed. For others, say tomboys who grow up to be heterosexual, cis-gendered women, their early expressions of gender variance are part of a struggle with the narrow scope of conventional womanhood. And finally, there are children who may experiment wildly with gender and sexuality their whole lives rather than experiencing their gender identities as part of a process that gets resolved, stabilized, or completed.

While Meadow's observations about the transgender child develop out of research on the parents of trans* children, I am less interested in the specific experiences of a generation of gender-questioning people and more intrigued by the logics and protocols of representation that impact how, when, and under what conditions the trans* body becomes legible, recognizable, and even lovable or desirable.

If an earlier generation of "queer" children grew up in households where they were viewed with suspicion or fear or dislike—and that is the plot of both *Ma Vie en Rose* and *Tomboy*—or if earlier generations of trans* young adults of color took refuge in households where they could remake the very meaning of family—as in *Paris Is Burning*—current generations might grow up within a system that, rather than despising transgender bodies, sees them as miniaturized adults taking a somewhat different path to normative maturation. In this model, the child and the adult are coherent wholes, with one mapping across time and space onto the other, a process that allows for belief in totalities, completeness, identities, and fixed coordinates for self and other. But what if we understood identification, kinship, and desire as partial, incomplete, evolving? And what if we situated the trans* child not as an alternative route to manhood or womanhood but as the gateway to a different understanding of generational transmission, as a symbol of inevitably eccentric versions of embodiment produced alongside traditional performances of gender stability, and as a rupture in ideological flow?

The refusal to see parts as merely the micro articulations of the whole offers us the possibility of seeing trans* bodies differently—not as bodies out of sync with the gender logics of their social environments, but potentially as bodies whose parts, particularly their genitalia but also their musculature, their fleshy areas, their protrusions and their flatness, their parts that hang and their parts that retract, all mean something other than what the logic of gender dictates. This view of the trans* body is one that we can access using the merographic model of kinship described by Marilyn Strathern in her 1992 book *After Nature: English Kinship in the Late Twentieth Century.*[9] Here Strathern advocates for seeing kinship as a set of fragmented and partial relations rather than as a holistic system in which intact families give rise to coherence and clear lines of descent. Strathern's work is a crucial part of remapping kinship under the pressure of not only trans* bodies in heteronormative households but also IVF technologies and new modes of reproductive technologies.

As photographer and gender theorist Del LaGrace Volcano's early work in *Sublime Mutations* on trans* bodies and their altered genitalia proposed, libidinal impulses are constantly being rewritten by the shifting physical and discursive forms and shapes of the bodies that surround us.[10] And so, while the parental activism around transgender children attempts to ensure that their "different" children remain recognizable to the parents and teachers and other kids in their orbits, trans* activists and image makers are trying to draw attention not only to the shifting parameters of the body but also to changing protocols of kinship, shifting libidinal landscapes, and new practices of association, identification, coalition, and desire. As Joe Latham puts it, trans* bodies challenge the nature of reality itself: "Transsexuality is a productive site for understanding how sex is made in medicine and how this shapes what is possible, not only for trans people who seek medical interventions, but more widely."[11]

Even as straight families reorient their trans-curious children toward normative adulthoods and away from connections with transsexual, transgender, and transitioning adults, they nevertheless seem to install in those children a sense of jeopardy and danger. And so contemporary young trans* activists simultaneously express an unquestioned sense of their own legitimacy *and* the need for safe space and trigger warnings. As we shall see in the next chapter, the clash between an enduring sense of legitimacy, on the one hand, and entitlement installed by supportive but normative parents, on the other, not only disrupts the history of trans* exclusions and anti-trans* violence that young trans* people learn about in college but also creates odd and contradictory impulses among privileged trans* youth. Sometimes young trans* people want to protest all narratives about trans* life that show transphobic violence, and at other times they want to distance themselves from trans* issues altogether.

When trans* youth route their desires through their parents rather than through older trans* activists, they become part of a more or less seamless transition from trans* youth to gender-normative adulthood. But reminders of earlier eras of transgender aspiration cannot be so easily eradicated. Consider, for example, British queer photographer Sara Davidmann's extraordinary project on trans* life, *Ken. To Be Destroyed,* which she created from papers she found among her mother's belongings after her death.[12] This project reminds us of what gets lost in the rush to recognize, definitively classify, and thus solidify the shifting ground of trans* identifications. But it also reaches across generations for an ambiguous gender-queer figure who cannot be understood from the perspective of present tense renderings of transgender identity.

The project begins with a manila envelope on which the words "Ken. To be destroyed" have been written and which contain letters between Sara's mother and her sister Hazel, Ken's wife, about Ken's (or K's) desire to be a woman. The letters span the years 1953–2003 and include correspondence with medical professionals about hormone treatments. There is also a cache of photographs, which Sara uses to tell a story about a life not lived. Although Sara had known about her uncle from her mother, she had not see these letters or photos and so had no sense of the impact K's admission had on the married life she shared with Hazel.

After getting her siblings' grudging permission, Davidmann began to work with the documents, not only to create a record of presence but also to offer an account of absence, loss, and denial. The aesthetic work that Davidmann performs on these texts and images calls attention both to ways in which bodies are inscribed within the family and to the many casual forms of erasure that normativity demands. *Ken. To Be Destroyed* is suggestive and elliptical, full of silence, secrecy, holes, and echoes. Like the case of Juana Aguilar that I discussed earlier, this archive reminds us that gender-ambiguous figures from earlier historical periods cannot be explained using the contemporary language of transgender identity.

Every photograph in this complex archive gives evidence of multiple realities. In a wedding photo, the joy of the bride is matched by the oddly grim or confused look on the groom's face; he seems to be flinching away from the camera, from the bride, from the wedding, from proof itself. Hard evidence of lives lived otherwise is hard to find. As Marianne Hirsch puts it in an essay on family photographs: "Photographs offer a prism through which to study the postmodern space of cultural memory composed of leftovers, debris, single items that are left to be collected and assembled in many ways, to tell a variety of stories, from a variety of often competing perspectives."[13]

Hazel and Ken, Sara tells us early on in her catalogue essay, "lived in Edinburgh, and after K's death (1979) and Hazel's (2003), they were buried side by side in a graveyard there." They were married side by side and slept side by side and lived side by side and were buried sided by side. This image echoes the sentiments expressed by Maggie Nelson in *The Argonauts* as she accompanies her trans\* partner, Harry, on the journey that for him has no specific destination. As noted earlier, Nelson understands herself as a fellow traveler, "undergoing transformations beside each other."[14] Maybe this is how Hazel felt about K, maybe not. Maybe she felt abandoned by her husband; maybe she felt unrecognized as a woman; maybe she also had a secret, as married people do. In one of the last photographs in the series, Sara reimagines K as a bride and situates him side by side with Hazel. Here K is the mirror image of Hazel and they appear in a sisterly relation. Perhaps we can use this concept of side by sideness or adjacency to think about the parallel lives of people who cross, pass, hide.

*Ken. To Be Destroyed* offers a number of different perspectives on trans* generations. First, the project reminds viewers that identity categories shift and change over time, such that "transgender" today may barely belong in the same category as the "gender variant" of just twenty, thirty, or forty years ago. Furthermore, the photographs of K and Hazel, and the absence from the archives of all kinds of images, offer a different understanding of the violence endured by trans* people. We recognize through this project that violence can take the form of gentle coercion into the category of belonging; or it can operate through inclusion rather than exclusion, or through silence rather than hate speech. Perhaps we need a broader palette for talking and thinking about harm, vulnerability, pain, and destruction. A project such as *Ken. To Be Destroyed* offers a more nuanced model for thinking about jeopardy—it is not that K was bashed or physically harmed but that she was situated on the wrong side of reality. Finally, as we see in this project, recuperation is always also violent and complicit, and so, when we retrieve the lost biography of a trans* woman, we simultaneously unmake the story of his wife and possibly we settle too quickly on the meaning of Ken/K's cross-identification. Indeed, when presenting this work publicly, I often have been asked about my choice to alternate my use of pronouns for K. The sense that audience members have conveyed in these questions is that K's identity is settled as female and should be addressed as such. My point here is that K enters into representation only under the sign of destruction ("Ken, To Be Destroyed") and thus the fluctuating pronoun captures the way that K flickers in and out of historical recognition. Settling on "she" will not rescue K; it will not resolve the danger she faced and it will not provide a truer portrait of who she was.

The danger in all attempts to figure out these emotional economies of survival lies in the impulse to balance the books, to make everything add up. But some accounts are not so easy to settle, and in fact, in trying to settle them, we may pay too high a price for coherence.

As Saidiya Hartman puts it in an essay on navigating the archives of brutality that make up the history of slavery, we have to ask why we want to tell the story of those who left either no trace or at best only mottled marks of their existence—crossed-out narratives and scrubbed photographic surfaces. And that is the question: when we try to tell a narrative about those who have been lost to gross brutality or subtle erasure, do we do it for them or for ourselves? Hartman, in "Venus in Two Acts," settles on a methodology that deploys "narrative restraint" or "the refusal to fill in the gaps and provide closure."[15]

Sometimes we need more narrative, sometimes less. Sometimes the adult from an older generation of trans* identification offers a necessary portal to a young person struggling to inhabit a body that does not fit. Sometimes that same vector of identification blocks the young person's ability to articulate identity for themself. Returning to *Paris Is Burning,* we can perhaps appreciate the creative work that went into making, occupying, and sustaining the ball families and the houses and the many generations of trans* people to whom they offered and still today offer a home, love, and support. Such families, "united in a mutual bond," seem less fragile than the middle-class households that cluster around their trans* children offering them summer camps, counseling, and literature to read. And while contemporary middle-class households might install in their kids a sense of jeopardy, less protected households offer instead survival skills. In *Paris Is Burning,* Dorian Corey compared the houses to street gangs and proposed that drag and the realness of the queens' performances might allow them to walk home unmolested at night. In precarious queer communities of color, kinship is less a tidy system of alliances and blood and more a scrappy support system designed to offer sustenance in a world where the police are not your protection but rather the source of your vulnerability. And *Paris Is Burning* needs to be situated within the context of the multiple sites where queer people of color create kinship in order to survive a world hostile to their very existence. In this sense, we might think about trans* people in prison who participate in prison families and pass on information to each other about how to survive in the criminal justice system.

Miss Major, an executive director of the Trans, Gender Variant, and Intersex Justice Project (TGIJP),[16] is a Black, transgender woman who has spent time incarcerated and who is now a fierce activist focused on the abuse of transgender people in prison, particularly women. Miss Major is also the "mama" of a group within TGIJP called Make It Happen Mamas (MIHM), dedicated to building mentorship programs for younger transgender women of color. This idea of a prison family and its extension beyond the jail offers a very different understanding of kinship than those models that revolve around the middle-class family and its needs. Transgender women of color, Miss Major points out, are outside mainstream LGBT politics and on the wrong side of justice: "One of the things that happens for a girl getting involved in the PIC [prison industrial complex] is we already, from the moment we decided to be a transgendered person, are living outside the law."[17]

Trans* men of color (some are transgendered, some are butches, some are perceived as masculine) are also subject to increased rates of incarceration in comparison to white transgender men and butches. As Sarah Haley's book *No Mercy Here* details, the widespread perception of Black bodies, and no doubt other female bodies of color, as masculine or improperly gendered leads to the criminalization of many transmasculine people of color.[18] In an essay titled "Out of Compliance," on masculine-identified people in women's prisons, Lori Girshick notes that many of the gender-nonconforming people she spoke to in women's prisons identified with the term "aggressive" or "stud" rather than "lesbian" or "transgender." Some of the people she spoke to also used the term "tomboy," and some identified as transgender men. For these masculine-identified people, the prison was a place where femininity was enforced and their "aggressive" demeanors were deemed violent, criminal, or dangerous. These folks are forced to wear tight clothing with feminine lines and T-shirts and panties that enact what one prison calls "forced feminization."[19]

One butch African American prisoner, Kris Shelley, has been in prison for nine years. Shelley, who calls themself a "gender-nonconforming lesbian," was moved from juvenile hall to prison at the age of seventeen. Shelley was incarcerated for a robbery that they committed with another person, an Asian male; because Shelley was carrying an unloaded gun, they received a twelve-year sentence, while their co-defendant received three years. In jail, Shelley was widely perceived by the guards to be dangerous and was routinely humiliated for their gender appearance and savaged by the male guards with pepper spray and batons. Shelley explains that the only way they could avoid the violent treatment was to become compliant, passive, and demure. In their words: "Then all of a sudden I grew up and learned how to become quiet and humble and not bite into their words. That's when they finally left me alone."[20]

In thinking about queer generations and the very different experiences of white trans* people and trans* people of color over time, across space, and in and out of various institutional settings (school, family, prison, hospital), we see how, as Stephen Dillon states, "the US prison regime works with race, gender, space, and mobility to structure regimes of knowledge—not only how we understand the forces that bring us into being, but also, quite literally, what we are able to know."[21] As Dillon proposes, certain epistemologies of the closet, the family, the home, and the school show us a version of U.S. culture in which trans* people find liberatory potential in the recognitions bestowed upon them by parents, teachers, coworkers, and intimates. But this vision of American freedom is underwritten by a whole set of other mechanisms of recognition and surveillance that shuttle trans* people of color, often women, often sex workers, between various forms of criminalization, policing, and incarceration.

Perhaps one important difference between middle-class models of kinship, family, and cross-generational transmission and those that operate within other communities has to do with the function of friendship. The small gender outlaws in the families that Tey Meadow studies operate mostly within worlds where they are the only trans* people in family and possibly within their immediate communities. And even in Davidmann's text, the gender-variant subject appears solo. The houses of the ball scene ripple with fierce friendships by comparison and offer community that stretches far beyond biological kinship.

I offer a final example here of kinship beyond the family in the form of a small film from 2015 that built an understanding of trans* kinship and community out of the raw material of friendship. *Tangerine,* directed by Sean Baker and shot on the iPhone 5s, a new platform and a small screen, was committed to capturing not a grand narrative about "the transsexual" but multiple complex "small" narratives of trans* life in the city, all of which add up to counternarratives of life, death, community, freedom, and mobility. It starred two first-time trans* actresses, Kitana Rodriguez and Mya Taylor, playing transgender sex workers, Sin-Dee Rella and Alexandra, in east Hollywood. Hollywood here, in an ironic dig at mainstream cinema, references not the film industry but the gritty, grim, strip malls populated by hucksters by day and hustlers by night. The film is revolutionary because it breaks with the protocols for representing trans* bodies, within both negative and positive paradigms, focusing instead on friendship, sex work, conflict, failure, and disappointment, and it does so with humor and verve. *Tangerine* shows trans* sex workers under the watchful eye of the law striving to preserve a friendship, to avenge an infidelity, and to make a little cash and a little art. Alexandra and Sin-Dee struggle with wit and resilience against the indignities of everyday life. While the police are ever present in the film—on the corners, in cruisers, a phone call away—and while the prison is both past and future, the women use their alliance to produce a life that is more than the sum of their wounds and injuries.

While the film does not usher us into the post-abolitionist utopia that some label a "beautiful impossibility,"[22] they do experience small moments of triumph in which other worlds can be glimpsed. In a quiet and moving scene that might be considered utopian, Alexandra pays the owner of a local bar to let her perform. She pressures Sin-Dee to accompany her to her big performance, and against all odds—and despite having to spend time kidnapping and subduing a woman who Sin-Dee thinks is sleeping with her man—Alexandra ends up on the stage in a red dress crooning "Toyland" à la Doris Day. In the time-space of the film, it is Christmas Eve, and this song about a "mystic merry place" conjures a childhood past filled with toys and joy that certainly the main characters in the film have not had and cannot look back on. In Doris Day's version of the song, Toyland is the space of childhood pleasure, and once its boundaries are breached and the child begins to grow up, they can never access it again. For Alexandra and Sin-Dee, Toyland is, to quote the late queer theorist José Muñoz, a place and a feeling that are "visible only in the horizon." It is a future and not a past, a form of queer visuality that is still to come. "To access queer visuality," Muñoz writes, "we may need to squint, to strain our vision and force it to see otherwise, beyond the limited vista of the here and now."[23]

When the camera pulls back from Alexandra's luminous performance, we see that Sin-Dee is struggling with the waitress over getting drinks, and the club is empty except for a few people at the bar. The tension between the space of the song, the shimmery light that shines down on Alexandra as she performs, and the harsh light of the bar in which Sin-Dee is moved, angered, and struggling all at once, captures the challenge of attending to the lives of trans* people, lives lived one minute at the edge of utopian possibility and the next in despair at the return of the ordinary.

This small film, focused on the fears, hopes, defeats, and small triumphs in a night in the life of trans women, succeeds by avoiding triumphalism. The micro scale of the iPhone does not diminish the lives that it captures, nor does it represent them as small in relation to other, grander lives and love. Rather, the small screen alerts us to how much we miss when we see life represented back to us only on the big screen, only according to the logic of heroism, progress, and achievement.

The goal here then is not to shoehorn eccentric bodies into already existing systems of rule, governance, pleasure, and punishment. The pursuit of trans* worlds means shattering the realities within which those trans* bodies require recognition, rights, and accommodations. As trans* activists say about prison, it is not about finding space in the prison that is appropriate for trans bodies; we should instead be using the occasion of the crisis initiated by the trans* body to question the practice of caging humans in the first place. In other words, there is no right cage. In an essay titled "Building an Abolitionist Trans and Queer Movement with Everything We've Got," scholar activists Morgan Bassichis, Alexander Lee, and Dean Spade chart the suppression of radical queer agendas in the twenty-first century in favor of assimilationist projects that promote marriage, securitization, conventional family, and tax benefits. They describe multiple tactics that communities might adopt instead of succumbing to the easy path of inclusion and recognition (e.g., embracing liberation as a collective process; engaging in trickle-up change; looking for security through "collective transformation," not more police), and they conclude by arguing that we orient away from the reasonable, the pragmatic, and the possible in favor of the utopian, the fantastical, and the impossible: "What would it mean," they ask," to *embrace,* rather than *shy away from,* the impossibility of our ways of living as well as our political visions? What would it mean to desire a future that we can't even imagine but that we are told couldn't ever exist?"[24] It is this impossible vision of a world that we are told cannot exist that becomes the utopian goal of thinking trans* generationally.

Using the concept of impossibility and even trans* "unrealities"—unrealized worlds that limn our own, unreal embodiments that do not seek ratification, unrealizable modes of being that by exceeding contemporary framings, challenge them—we might turn away from the pragmatics of recognition and identification and look instead to the way older generations of trans* people lived and survived in the realms of the inauthentic, the unfaithful, and the unverifiable. They did so not in the hope of one day being recognized as real but because the violence of the real was not worth the price of admission. In turn, the lessons these older trans* people have to offer to younger people struggling to balance the demands of visibility, inclusion, and acceptance with their own revolutionary desires to change everything are invaluable. While some privileged trans* youth are encouraged to become "normal" as they grow into the adulthoods meticulously curated for them by their parents, many other trans* young people will reject such futures in favor of new paradigms of life, love, and family.

# FIVE

# Trans* Representation

Transgender is a shape.

Jeanne Vacarro, "Feelings and Fractals" (2015)

A few years ago I attended a queer, transnational performance studies conference where a play was staged about a queer historical figure. This figure greatly resembled the gender-ambiguous Juana Aguilar, researched by María Elena Martínez, whom I discussed earlier. And indeed, the play, staged by Mexican performance artist Jesusa Rodríguez, was based on Martínez's research. Rather than receiving the play as an interesting piece of period theater, audience members became irate and angered by the depiction, especially since some parts of the life of the hermaphroditic character were played for comedic effect. The conference turned, overnight, from a wildly imaginative series of performances, talks, and theatre productions into a somber event filled with roundtables, short tables, long tables, and turned tables on what had gone wrong with this representation of a "transgender" figure. The dramaturg was accused of transphobia, historical reference points were thrown to the wind, and many tears were shed. I later wrote a blog in response to what I had seen, and I linked the event and the hard feelings it produced to calls for trigger warnings and protests that targeted queer cultural producers rather than homophobes and transphobes. My essay was received enthusiastically at first, but it quickly became obvious that my piece was the journalistic equivalent of waving a red flag at a rampaging bull. People accused me of all manner of perfidy, and one wit dubbed me the "sports dad of queer theory" for my grumpy attitude toward "the kids today."

Since then there have been other, similar, transgender protests of queer representation. I end this chapter with one such example, in an attempt to see what we can make of these battles over the project of representing trans\* bodies. My goal is not at all to chastise young people or tut-tut about how young people have lost the plot on political engagement. After all, I am not a particularly skilled or dynamic activist myself. Rather, my goal has long been to try to understand the visual protocols for representing the trans\* body, trans\* experience, and trans\* identity, be it in texts that are positive or negative, abstract or realistic. It is generally a good idea not to approach the visual materials documenting trans\* life with a moral framework that leads only to adjudication; instead, we are better served by considering the formal methods by which trans\* experience can be represented and the benefits and liabilities therein.

In my 2005 book *In a Queer Time and Place: Transgender Bodies, Subcultural Lives* I argued that the regular temporal frameworks that organize life expectations in Euro-American contexts were themselves part and parcel of a normalizing system that orients diverse communities with heterogeneous desires toward a remarkably narrow swath of life narratives. Those orderly and predictable life narratives become the stuff of all kinds of governmental logics of rule and make possible everything from inheritance claims to insurance algorithms. If we situate queerness as a contrary temporal logic, we begin to see how and where and why certain bodies are perceived as threatening, destabilizing, and aberrant. Reading queerness as an altered relation to time and place also takes us out of the ambit of stable social identities and provides a non-identitarian language for social, sexual and political eccentricity. In this chapter I ask about the visual language that captures queerness, transitivity and trans* identities across variables understandings of time and space.

Since I wrote *In a Queer Time and Place,* many other books have emerged on queer temporality. Elizabeth Freeman's widely read *Time Binds: Queer Temporalities, Queer Histories,* for example, theorizes a queer history that can be found in "nonsequential time," an erotic temporality that inheres to discontinuity, a "body's microtemporalities," and the libidinal pull of the anachronistic.[1] Similarly, Lee Edelman has used the notion of queer time to make visible the mostly hidden logics of political structures that draw us into hackneyed and normative formulations of self and politics by situating the future itself as a function of reproductive normativity.[2] In a critique of Edelman's rallying cry of "no future," the late José Esteban Muñoz, in *Cruising Utopia,* conjured the (im)possibility of "Brown futures," offering instead a queer phenomenological vision of utopian horizons that allow for the possibility that "we are not yet queer" and that queerness is very much still to come.[3] More recently, this conjuring of a queer future has preoccupied Black queer scholars such as Kara Keeling and Tavia Nyong'o, who have reminded us of the difference that race makes to the ways in which we imagine futurity, the archaic, the child, spoiled pasts, intransigent presents, and so on.[4]

As part of the first wave of books on queer temporality, mine laid out the implications of a model of queerness that is not simply about what kinds of bodies have sex with what kinds of bodies, but about different life narratives, alternative ways of being in relation to others, and new practices of occupying space. For example, I proposed that we might privilege friendship networks over extended families when assessing the structures of intimacy that sustain queer lives, and we might also think about transgenderism in particular as not simply a contrapuntal relationship between bodily form and content but as an altered relation to seeing and being seen. Transgenderism, in other words, has never been simply a new identity among many others competing for space under the rainbow umbrella. Rather, it constitutes radically new knowledge about the experience of being in a body and can be the basis for very different ways of seeing the world.

This is, at least in part, one of the arguments Kara Keeling makes in her work on race and transgender visuality. In an essay titled "Looking for M——: Queer Temporality, Black Political Possibility, and Poetry from the Future," Keeling fuses a theory of anticolonial temporality gleaned from Fanon with an understanding of the experience of cinematic affect taken from Deleuze to situate Black trans* futurity as something that exceeds the knowledge of conventional documentary film. Keeling develops this argument in "Looking for M——" to propose the appearance in Black film of an "impossible possibility," or worlds and modes of being that escape "recognition, meaning, and valuation." In Daniel Peddle's film *The Aggressives* (2005), a Black trans* character named M disappears and the filmmaker is unable to track hir down. For Keeling, *The Aggressives* provided a template for the dis-appearance of gender-queer Black bodies. M's disappearance within the arc of the film is not simply unfortunate or even tragic, it is rather a "political act" that resists the narrative closure which the film tries to impose on unruly lives and, just as importantly, refuses the classifications of LGBT by turning to the subcultural designation of "aggressives," a term that does not neatly match up with L, G, B, or T. Keeling's theoretically innovative reading disrupts the easy narratives of gender-variant lives that would place very different life narratives alongside each other under the headings of queer or trans and across time and space.

If, as Keeling's work has shown, bodies often exceed the apparatuses (medical, cinematic, narrative, or social) available to represent them, what methods *should* we use to track the disorderly histories of trans*? We also need to remember Sandy Stone's important intervention in her "Posttranssexual Manifesto" from over twenty years ago. Stone argued against the standard narratives of transsexual identity that had been advanced by doctors, psychiatrists, feminists, and anthropologists, insisting instead on the importance of transsexuals self-representing and refusing to be the object of knowledge. Commenting on some popular accounts of transsexual life written by nontranssexuals—notably Gary Kates's work on Chevalier d'Éon and Anne Bolin's early ethnographies of "traversing gender"—Stone writes: "Both Kates' and Bolin's studies are in most respects excellent work, and were published in the same collection as an earlier version of this essay; but still there are no subjects in these discourses, only homogenized, totalized objects—fractally replicating earlier histories of minority discourses in the large. So when I speak the forgotten word, it will perhaps wake memories of other debates. The word is *some*."[5] The fragmentation, segmentation, multiplicity of the category trans* can only emerge within an optic that recognizes trans* as a capacious and fluid category rather than a diagnosis.

Seeing trans* bodies differently, then—not simply as trans bodies that provide an image of the nonnormative against which normative bodies can be discerned, but as bodies that are fragmentary and internally contradictory, bodies that remap gender and its relations to race, place, class, and sexuality, bodies that are in pain or that represent a play of surfaces, bodies that sound different than they look, bodies that represent palimpsestic relations to identity—means finding different visual, aural, and haptic codes through which to figure the experience of being in a body. After all, the trans* body is not so easy to represent, and the visual frame that captures such bodies either has to reveal sites of contradiction on the gender-variant body (through nakedness perhaps, which risks sensationalizing such bodies) or through other kinds of exposure, violent, intrusive, or otherwise.

Jeanne Vacarro has offered the experience of touch as an alternative method for reading trans* bodies; she describes, under the heading "Handmade," a logic of knowing that departs totally from the diagnostic forms of classification that have mediated trans* people's ability to say who they are. Vacarro writes: "If we are to dislodge transgender from the event of its medicalization and meditate, alternatively, on the handmade dimensionality of experience, what might transgender come to mean? ... The handmade is a haptic, affective theorization of the transgender body, a mode of animating material experience and accumulative felt matter. As bodily feeling and sensation transform flesh parallel to diagnostic and administrative forces, a handmade orientation foregrounds the work of crafting identity."[6] This is a gorgeous understanding of embodiment through the world-making activities of craft and crafting, and it opens out onto visual methodologies deployed by various artists for representing without fetishizing bodies that might either seamlessly pass or seem lodged between the systems of representation that promise to deliver orderly arrangements of binary gender to viewing audiences whose sense of visual pleasure depends on such tidy systems. The haptic offers one path around the conundrum of a binary visual plane (what is not male appears to be female, what is not female appears to be male).

Indeed, the haptic offers a great aesthetic frame for trans* representation in general. As explained by theorist Laura Marks in her book *Touch,* the haptic is a sensory mode of perception that engages a model of knowing and perception that is not oriented toward mastery, not deployed simply at the level of the visual. The haptic both names the way the mind grasps for meanings that elude it while still holding on to the partial knowledge available. It violates the opposition between subject and object and demands that the viewer/namer/authority feel implicated in the act of looking, naming, and judging. For Marks, the haptic is "a visual erotics that offers its object to the viewer but only on condition that its unknowability remain intact, and that the viewer, in coming closer, give up his or her own mastery."[7] As this quote indicates, hapticality organizes meaning, knowing, and seeing in ways that exceed rational, sense-making enterprises and instead force the viewer to examine their own relations to truth and authenticity. This is a perfect frame for the trans* body, which, in the end, does not seek to be seen and known but rather wishes to throw the organization of all bodies into doubt.

A great example of haptic work on trans* bodies that points to new forms of embodiment without seeking to know or master them can be found in the outlandish sculptures, goofy drawings, and loopy films by trans* artist Harry Dodge.[8] His work partakes wholeheartedly and joyfully in the haptic while performing a practice given over to humor, hybridity, and exploration of the unnameable. He identifies the unnamable in an interview as "anti-authoritarian leakage, overflow, and profusion."⁹ His sculptures, made from discarded materials, trash, and found objects and materials, capture beautifully this other language for embodiment—a play of surfaces, a humorous engagement with being, a flirtation with becoming, a reckoning with the "dynamic indeterminacy" that trans\* bodies point to and inhabit, narrate, and even historicize. In some of Dodge's work, cheery objects point and wave to one another, and in drawings Dodge creates cartoonlike scenes within which hybrid but allegorical bodies speak in poetic ways to each other. In the pencil drawing "Lobster Boy (regarding articulation)," for example, a boyish figure holds up his gigantic claw of a hand and thinks: "The spirit of if I had each of my separate fingers lives in my heart." Meanwhile, another figure, perhaps a rock, counters: "There's not a name for everything." This drawing is fantastical, imaginative, and hilarious. It opposes the desire to grasp meaning with the impossibility of naming, situating unknowability in many forms of able and disabled embodiment, not just the gender variable. The haptic, which describes a mode of sensing through touch, lives in the massive claw hands, in their pointing mechanisms, and in the rock's pronouncement about unnameability. In visual artist Micha Cárdenas's performances, too, the haptic frames the trans\* body, in the form of wearable electronics, immersive virtual environments, and various forms of hacktivism and new media productive of what she calls "transrealities."¹⁰

Scholars like Jeanne Vacarro have offered the language of the haptic as an alternative to the medical, the legal, and the mediatized will to know and as a remapping of the gendered body, not around having or lacking the phallus but around manipulating and knowing via the hand, the finger, the arm, the body in bits and pieces. The haptic body and the haptic self are not known in advance but improvised over and over on behalf of a willful and freeing sense of bewilderment.

Taking the haptic as well as the sense of queer temporality and the unnameable and unknowable experience of embodiment as our foundation, let's examine how trans* bodies have been represented over the past two decades—what kinds of contestations have emerged about these representations—and then think through some indefinite, nonspecific, and open-ended approaches to trans* representation.

In the late 1990s and early 2000s, some films were in circulation that took the transgender body as their topic or that deployed the transgender body as a metaphor for other unstable forms of identity. But most films featuring trans* identities still cast transgenderism as a kind of aberration, as something in need of explanation, or as a symbol for illegible social identities. That said, in the 1990s mainstream cinema parted ways with the tendency to represent transgender people as mad, bad, and dangerous. Films like Brian De Palma's *Dressed to Kill* from 1980, not to mention Alfred Hitchcock's *Psycho* from 1960, had made the connection between gender variance and serial murder seem obvious and inevitable. But that changed when three different films shifted the protocols for conventional cinematic representations of transgender lives.

*THE CRYING GAME*, DIRECTED BY NEIL JORDAN (1992)   In some films, but most notably in Neil Jordan's *The Crying Game*, the transgender body came to serve as a metaphor for other sites of instability and for the fraught and contradictory sets of political commitments that accumulate around and through race, nation, and class. In this film, the trans* character Dil (Jaye Davidson) provides an occasion for an extended discourse on appearance and reality, the Irish Republican Army (IRA) versus English nationalism, and racist and transphobic fetishism. For all its fetishistic looking at the Black trans* body, however, the film did manage to situate transgenderism within a larger political and social context and as part of an ongoing revolutionary project. The story involves a Black English soldier, Jody (Forest Whitaker), kidnapped by IRA members Fergus (Stephen Rea) and Jude (Miranda Richardson), who dies while trying to escape, but not before he forms a bond with Fergus and asks him to visit his girlfriend, Dil, in London. Fergus follows through on his promise, and the subsequent encounter leads to romance and the revelation of her transgenderism.

Despite Fergus's revulsion when he confronts Dil's "incomplete" transition—namely, her penis—the film allows a learning curve for the main characters. Fergus and Dil learn what Jody had already known, namely that all forms of nationalism require fictions of the natural, the communal, and the unified, when in fact the only thing holding people together is fear and violence. In this configuration, each character finds themself both inside and outside of national belonging, and Dil's mismatched body becomes a symbol for the patchwork of social contradictions that nationalisms attempt to smooth over. The film also highlighted erotic tensions between the transgender woman and the cis-gender man, and while Fergus's first reaction to Dil's embodiment was revulsion, the film tracks an unorthodox trajectory for his desire, within which neither Dil's gender nor Fergus's sexual orientation is definitively fixed.

BOYS DON'T CRY, DIRECTED BY KIM PEIRCE (1999)  *Boys Don't Cry* by Kim Peirce is the breakthrough film for thinking about the trans* body as simultaneously viable and vulnerable, sexy and powerful. This film about the real-life murder of a trans*masculine youth, Brandon Teena, was sensitive to the ambiguity of Brandon Teena's embodiment and expansive on his desires and gender practices.

In my earlier readings of the film, I accounted for a "transgender gaze" within which time, space, desire, and embodied identification all splinter, representing a collapse of the matrices of gender and sexuality.[11] While certain shots through a car's windshield give viewers a sense of the beauty and desolation of the Nebraska landscape, jump cuts collapse time and space, fantasy and reality, reminding us that the trans* body not only asks that we slow down the lightning-fast calculations by which we assign genders to bodies, but also stalls systems of signification that attach masculinity to maleness, femininity to femaleness, leaving nothing in between. In *Boys Don't Cry,* the murder of Brandon Teena, whose gender has been recognized by the young woman he loves but not by her family and friends, represents the shattered and uneven nature of the reception of trans* visuality. The film eloquently conjures the shared vision of the trans* person and their lover, even as it confronts the violence that seeks to destroy that vision.

In my original reading of the film, I noted how we move with this film from looking or staring at the transgender body to seeing the world through hir eyes. This is captured most effectively in a brutal sequence where Brandon is exposed by local men and where he momentarily leaves his body, allowing him to see himself being displayed. I then explored the cinematic techniques that allow viewers to participate in a "transgender gaze" or "glance." Experimental interludes in this film give us access, as viewers, not only to the experience of transgenderism—as a split, a contradiction (pleasurable or otherwise), a friction—but also to the experience of those who desire transgender people. The film made Brandon Teena into a cultural hero, a martyr, and a victim. Later I will recount what happened when a group of activists at a U.S. college, fifteen years after its release, understood *Boys Don't Cry* as a transphobic film organized around the dismantling of a young transsexual man's body.

*BY HOOK OR BY CROOK,* DIRECTED BY HARRY DODGE AND SILAS HOWARD (2001)   Finally, there is Dodge/Howard's brilliant independent film *By Hook or by Crook,* which focuses on trans* friendship, shared masculinities, the quest narrative, and road movie as a metaphor for transition and the nature of love in trans* contexts. This film was pioneering in terms of its ability to create a truly alternative vision while making no concessions to a straight viewer. *By Hook of by Crook* is the story of a friendship between two trans* masculine subjects. The transgender figures are just "he," with no explanation for their eccentric gendering given. Instead, the film highlights intimate bonds, sex, and love as the real themes of the film, showing the buddies on a quest that has no stable outcome; it is a road movie without an obvious destination. The quest functions instead as a metaphor for "continuous transition"—one of the features of trans* identity that makes it different from transsexualism. Here, the trans* character of Valentine in particular (played by Dodge) becomes a quixotic figure tilting not only at conventional gender norms but also at normative notions of family, sex, love, and belonging.

Looking at these films, one must remember and try to recreate the context in which they originally appeared. In the late 1990s and early 2000s transgenderism, and particularly transsexualism, was very much a focus of talk shows and media fascination. The media dealt with transsexuality as an exotic phenomenon for which the public was not ready. The mainstream media represented transgender people as "dysphoric," dishonest, disoriented, or worse, and this sense of disorientation, rather than being folded into a general postmodern condition, was cast as uninhabitable and pathologically unstable. Transgender bodies, indeed, represented a condition of radical instability against which other gendered identities appeared legible, knowable, and natural.

So far, I have argued that the representation of transgenderism depends on a repudiation of the veracity of the visual (passing), an embrace of the haptic (unknowing), and a narrative framework of continual transition (becoming). In earlier texts filmmakers and artists have used a number of techniques to visualize the trans\* body without reducing it to the binary template of male or female, and so we have witnessed the representation of the self as split (*Boys Don't Cry*), the representation of the body as inherently unstable and contradictory (*The Crying Game*), and the representation of the body as an absurd site that eludes linguistic and visual codes (*By Hook or by Crook* as well as Dodge's artwork). As a result of these pioneering efforts, contemporary filmmakers and television producers are neither trying to garner recognition of the trans\* body nor claiming it as exceptional. Influenced by the work of Jin Haritawarn, Riley Snorton, and Jasbir Puar on transnormalization, by Mel Chen on the materiality of grammar, and by Nikki Sullivan and others on the meaning of somatechnics, contemporary visual artists astutely rethink the intersections between technology, embodiment, identity, and biopolitical mechanisms of control.[12] In this way, in contemporary art and culture we can begin to rethink gender histories, the role of technology in reimagining the body and the interactions between bodies and landscapes/spaces, and dynamics of race, class, and ability.

In the contemporary landscape of representation, television has become more dominant than cinema; with its episodic structure and evolving plot lines, TV series allow for much more information and contradiction to enter into the representation of complex lives. An excellent example for our purposes is *Transparent* (2014–present), created and directed by Jill Soloway. In its first season, *Rolling Stone* credited it with "making the world safer for trans people"; *Out* dubbed it the first show to handle properly not only transgenderism but also bisexuality; and the *Advocate* called *Transparent,* simply, "great television."[13] Telling the story of a dysfunctional Jewish family in Los Angeles that falls apart and regroups around the patriarch's revelation of her transition from male to female, *Transparent* covers new ground for television. The refusal to trade only in positive images of trans people, never mind Jews, lesbians, female rabbis, and butch security guards, makes it unique in the media history of queer representation. Though less avant-garde than Dodge/Howard's work, *Transparent* nonetheless builds upon the carefully crafted trans\* regimes of representation that came before it. (Indeed, Silas Howard is a regular director of episodes of *Transparent.*) The series showcases some new techniques of representation in relation to the transgender body. And as in Sara Davidmann's text *Ken. To Be Destroyed* (examined in chapter 4), the narrative of the trans\* body appears both in relation to contemporary Jewish life and under the sign of potential destruction.

The challenge for *Transparent* lies in its ability to represent a specific trans experience ("someness," in Sandy Stone's terms) without making it representative of *all* trans experience. The show manages to convey, with some subtlety, the relief of coming out, the stress of feeling exposed, the sadness of being late to the table. With a writing team that includes queer writer Ali Liebegott and consultants who include artists Zachary Drucker and Rhys Ernst, *Transparent* made the wise decision to work with trans people's *own* narratives rather than to cleave faithfully to Jill Soloway's autobiographical story. Soloway's experience with her father's transition still forms the spine of the piece, but it is rounded out with a clutch of other stories about aging, sexual experimentation, addiction, sibling tension, and so on. Aspects of this episodic TV series stand out from previous trans representations: it is not committed to repairing the negative facets of representations of transgenderism, for example, but it also refuses to situate the trans* body as a lonely and singular entity. Rather, the trans* characters (some of whom appear in the present, some in a Jewish past in prewar Berlin) all appear in relation to and firmly within real-world events. The appearance of trans* characters throughout the series also offers critiques of the family and of all idealized notions of community.

*Transparent* continuously flirts with the archive of negative representations of trans* life and identities. Thus, part of the framing of Maura, the trans-parent, is as a wealthy person who has been cloistered in privilege and whose trans* identity means something very different from those of the trans* women she meets out in the "community." In season three, for example, Maura staffs an LGBT crisis hotline, and after taking a call from a troubled queer trans* person of color, Elizah, she goes off on a wild goose chase to find and potentially "save" this woman. The script pillories this rescue mission, however, and it is Maura who ends up in the hospital, not the object of her ministrations.

*Transparent* beautifully shows how the bourgeois family expands to embrace its own, even when its "own" is an aging patriarch turned transwoman, and it gives audiences a warts-and-all view into trans* life. Indeed, perhaps because *Transparent* is a TV series, it has to produce and invest not only in characters who are basically good people, trying hard and forging new ground, but also in those who screw up, hurt each other, and take two steps back for every one step forward. The range of characters is far-ranging and complex, as in real life.

Some transgender audiences of *Transparent* have complained that neither Jill Soloway nor the actor playing Maura, Jeffrey Tambor, is transgender. Tambor himself, in accepting his second Emmy Award for the role, urged producers and directors to "give transgender talent a chance." Not only that, but "give them auditions. Give them their story. Do that. And also, one more thing, I would not be unhappy were I the last cisgender male playing a female transgender on television. We have work to do."[14]

*We have work to do.* In this extraordinarily self-aware speech, Tambor made excellent use of his position as perhaps one of the most beloved transgender characters in the history of visual representation. But transgender activists, never mind transgender actors, remain irritated, to say the least, by the long history of casting nontransgender actors in transgender roles. *Transamerica* starred Felicity Huffman as a preoperative transsexual woman; *The Dallas Buyers Club* starred Jared Leto as a trans woman with AIDS; and of course, *Boys Don't Cry* starred Hilary Swank as Brandon Teena, the young trans* masculine youth who was killed for passing as male.

In recent years, transgender audiences have become more and more incensed by the casting of nontransgender actors, and a number of skirmishes have broken out over this practice. These skirmishes are symptomatic of a deeply felt sense of the injustice of having one's life depicted by people who have benefited from the binary of normative and nonnormative genders. But these protests also misrecognize the longer arc of trans* representation, a trajectory I have tried to sketch here, and there is a tendency to try to adjudicate the injustice in relation not to new films and TV shows but to films like *Boys Don't Cry,* retroactively critiquing and calling for a reckoning with the way that visual culture has framed transgender life. While I am sympathetic to such attempts to address a history of unfair and often toxic representations, I also want to consider the many ways we can refuse, resist, and recast these visual mechanisms in the present. I therefore close this chapter with an account of an event that unites both some of the tensions expressed in chapter 4 about trans* generational conflict and new tensions over the representation of trans* lives in an age of social media.

The film *Boys Don't Cry* was made in 1999. It took years to research, fund, cast, and shoot; was released to superb reviews; and went on to garner awards and praise for the lead actor, Hilary Swank, and the young director, Kim Peirce, not to mention the film's production team led by Christine Vachon. The film was hard hitting, visually innovative, and marked a massive breakthrough in the representation of gender-variant bodies. While there were certainly debates about decisions that Peirce made within the film's narrative arc (the omission of the murder of an African American friend, Philip DeVine, at the same time that Brandon was killed), *Boys Don't Cry* was received at the time as a magnificent film honoring the life of a gender-queer youth and conveying cinematically a sense of the jeopardy of gender-variant experiences. It was also seen as a sensitive depiction of life in small-town U.S.A. Kim Peirce went on to speak widely about the film in public venues, explaining her relationship to the subject matter of gender variance, working-class life, and gender- based violence.

In a screening of the film in 2016, with Peirce as a speaker, younger audiences took offense at the film and accused the film-maker of making money off the representation of violence against trans people. This happened when Peirce showed up to speak at a special screening of the film at Reed College in Oregon, just days after the presidential election in November 2016. Unbeknownst to the organizers of the screening, student protesters had removed posters from around campus that advertised the film and lecture, and they arrived early to the cinema on the night of the screening to hang new posters. These posters voiced a range of reactions to the film, including "You don't fucking get it!" and "Fuck Your Transphobia!" as well as "Trans Lives Do Not Equal $$." To cap it all off, the sign hung on the podium read: "Fuck this cis white bitch"!! The protesters waited until after the film had screened (at Peirce's request), then entered the auditorium shouting, "Fuck your respectability politics," and yelling over her commentary. Peirce finally left the room. After establishing some ground rules for a discussion, Peirce returned, but the conversation again got out of hand, and finally a student yelled at Peirce: "Fuck you, scared bitch." At which point the protesters filed out and Peirce left campus.

This is an astonishing set of events to reckon with for those of us who remember the events surrounding Brandon Teena's murder, the debates in the months that followed over Brandon Teena's identity, and, later, the reception of the film itself. The murder of Brandon Teena spurred early transgender activists into action, and many showed up at the trial of his killers. Despite much discussion at the time about whether Brandon was "butch" or "transgender," queer and transgender audiences were mostly satisfied with the depiction of Brandon Teena in *Boys Don't Cry*. The film appealed to many audiences, queer and straight, and it continues to play around the world.

The accounts of this protest give evidence of enormous vitriol, much of it blatantly misogynist (the repeated use of the word "bitch," for example), directed at a queer, butch filmmaker, and they leave us with an enormous number of questions about representational dynamics, clashes between different historical paradigms of queer and transgender life, and the expression of queer anger that, instead of being directed at murderous enemies in the mainstream of American political life, has been turned onto independent filmmakers within the queer and LGBT communities. After this incident at Reed, I heard from other students that they, too, felt "uncomfortable" with the representations of transgender life and death in *Boys Don't Cry*.

How might we respond to these objections in ways that do not dismiss the feelings of the students but that ask for different relations to protest, to the reading of complex texts, and to how anger about transphobic and homophobic texts might be directed? Here are a few thoughts.

*We need to situate this film properly within the history of the representation of transgender characters.* At the time that Peirce made *Boys Don't Cry*, most films featured transgender people only as monsters, killers, sociopaths, or isolated misfits (e.g., *Psycho* [Hitchcock, 1960]; *Dressed To Kill* [de Palma, 1980]; *The Silence of The Lambs* [Demme, 1991]). Few treated transgender people with even a modicum of comprehension, and even fewer dealt with the transphobic environments that were part of heteronormative family life. Very few films prior to *Boys* focused on transgender masculinity at all, and when transgender male characters did appear in film, they were often depicted as women who passed as men for pragmatic reasons (, e.g., *The Ballad of Little Jo*, 1993) or as androgynous figures of whimsy (e.g., *Orlando*, 1992). *Boys Don't Cry* is the first film in history to build a credible story line around the credible masculinity of a credible trans-masculine figure. Period.

*We cannot always demand a perfect match between directors, actors, and the material in any given narrative.* As a masculine person from a working-class background who had experienced sexual abuse, Peirce identified strongly with the life and struggles of Brandon Teena. Peirce, though not a transgender man, is gender variant. The film she produced was sensitive to Brandon Teena's social environment, his gender identity, his hard upbringing, and his struggle to understand himself and to be understood by others. If Peirce told a story in which the transgender body was punished, she did so not in order to participate in that punishment but because it would have been dishonest to tell the story any other way. The violence he suffered stood, at the time, as emblematic of the many forms of violence that transgender people suffered, and it called on the audiences of the film to rebuke the world in which such violence was commonplace.

*Transgender actors should play transgender roles, but that is not always possible and certainly was a long shot at the time Peirce made her film.* Peirce conducted a national search for a trans-masculine actor for *Boys Don't Cry*. She did screen tests with many trans-identified people, and she ultimately gave the role to the best actor available who was credible as a young female-bodied person passing for male. That actor was Hilary Swank, best known at the time for her role in *The Next Karate Kid* and occasional appearances on *Buffy the Vampire Slayer.* It was vital to have a strong performer in the role of Brandon Teena, and Swank was cast accordingly. Also, why should a transgender actor only play transgender roles—shouldn't we be asking cis-gendered directors to cast transgender men and women as romantic leads, dramatic protagonists, superheroes, and so forth?

*We should not be asking for films to make detours around scenes of sexual violence; instead, we should be asking what we actually mean by violence in any given context.* In *Boys Don't Cry,* the rape scene was brutal, hard to shoot, hard to act in, and overall a difficult, emotionally draining piece of filmmaking. But it is also a crucial part of the film, a way of representing faithfully the brutal violence that at the time was meted out regularly to gender-nonconforming bodies, and it was true to the specific fate of Brandon Teena. The brutality of the rape also cuts in and out of scenes in the police station as Brandon Teena reports the rape. The police treat Brandon as a "girl" who must have been "pleased" by the attention of the young men, whom they consider normal, sexual subjects. Thus, the rape scene damns the police, highlights the role of violence in the enforcement of normativity, and draws the audience's sympathies to Brandon in a way that makes transphobia morally reprehensible.

When we target scenes of rape and sexual violence in independent films about historical characters and call them unwatchable, we are making it difficult to grapple with all kinds of historical material that involves systemic violence and oppression. But we are also limiting the meaning of "violence" to physical assault. As so many theorists have shown, violence can also appear in the form of civility, empathy, absence, indifference, and non-appearance.[15] Violence is the glue of contemporary representation: we regularly watch films in which cars are blown up (every film with a chase scene); planes are shot down (many films featuring Tom Cruise or James Bond); superheroes sweep the streets of evil, taking out hundreds of people at a time (*Iron Man* but also *Ghostbusters*); tidal waves destroy entire cities (*Deep Impact*); complete colonies of fish are swallowed up by marauding sharks (*Finding Nemo*); aliens land and eliminate buildings (*The War of the Worlds*); zombie mobs chase humans and slowly eat them (*The Walking Dead*)—and so forth and so on. To focus solely on sexual violence and ignore the more general context of cinematic violence, never mind taking complaints only to queer directors who are struggling to represent queer life rather than to straight directors ignoring queer and trans\* life, betrays a limited vision of representational systems and ideologies and ultimately leaves those systems and their biases completely intact.

The incident at Reed College offers an example of how hard it can be to share activist goals across different generations of people who experience their marginalized identities very differently and who may or may not be able to access and identify with the experiences of those who came before or after them. I offer the account of this screening and what followed not to mark it as outrageous or extraordinary but to highlight how central film and video were to struggles around visibility and viability in the 1990s and how more recently visual representation in the cinema has given way to the multi-platforms of social media. The material that, in the late years of the twentieth century, gave queer and trans\* people hope for easier days ahead today fuels anger and revulsion on the part of younger trans\* people and leads them to protest the very filmmakers who helped to create the privileges they currently enjoy. We can expect more such skirmishes in the future, given the rifts between generations of activists, but maybe the hinge of the * as it attaches to trans can be used to open up dialogue, difficult though it may be, rather than slam the door on further conversation.

# SIX

# Trans* Feminism

Transitioning is vibratory; transitioning women are,
first and most importantly, vibratory beings.

Eva Hayward, "Spider City Sex" (2010)

When I came out in 1980, some white feminists were waging war
on transsexuals, whom they saw as interlopers into spaces that
women had fought hard to protect from men. Separatism was a
thing, and women's bookstores and coffee shops and bars tried to
organize around a narrow politics of womanhood. Within such a
climate, it was hard to express gender variance of any kind, and
even as I embraced the sense of community that feminism
offered me, I felt confused by the emphasis on womanhood. In
the end I had to part ways with this version of feminism in order
to embrace my masculinity, and it took a long time for me find
my way back to a meaningful relation with gender politics.

I find my original frustration with a moralistic and women-
born-womyn-centered feminism echoed in the current antagonism that many transgender women voice against versions of
feminism that still insist on the centrality of female-bodied
women. The standoffs that took place in the early 2000s at the
annual Michigan Womyn's Music Festival (MWMF; see below)

between feminists defending "woman's land" and transwomen wanting to access that space brought some of this antagonism to a head, and new battlegrounds have since emerged in relation to "women's marches" following the election of Donald Trump to the presidency and shared spaces like public bathrooms.

Still, as we enter new eras of terror, and as social media networks continue to buzz with sexist, misogynist, and transphobic chatter, perhaps it is time to retire the old antagonisms and seek common ground. Feminist spaces cannot possibly be the only or the most fraught locations for transgender women, and many trans* men who come out as gay must surely have as much to say about misogyny in gay male communities. It is time to rethink the politics of trans* gender, the solidarities and antagonisms that allow people to work together or force them apart, and to consider whether the foundational binary of male-female may possibly have run its course. When the male-female binary crumbles, what new constellations of alliance and opposition emerge?

♀ ♀ ♂

Contemporary suspicion of feminism within transgender groups arises primarily from two sources: first, a strand of 1970s white feminism that found its loudest voice in a 1979 book by Janice Raymond titled *The Transsexual Empire;* and second, a more contemporary version of this antipathy found in the struggle over trans* women's acceptance (or lack thereof) at MWMF. Raymond's book was a deeply transphobic text, full of paranoid accusations about transsexual women invading and populating "womyn's space."[1] The language of empire in her title referred to the way in which she understood transsexuals to be colonizing womyn's work, bonds, functions, and domains. Raymond understood transsexual women to be literally invading, even "raping," female-born women, but she also, contradictorily, blamed transsexual women as complicit in the production, circulation, and consolidation of conventional femininity. The book was toxic; it also had considerable currency at the time.

The sentiments that Raymond expresses in *The Transsexual Empire* are reprehensible, without a doubt, yet they were representative of one small but vocal and fairly powerful group of women in the 1970s. Raymond's book should in no way be situated as representing *most* feminists' views on trans\* womanhood, then or now. Similarly, the rigidly exclusionary system of admission deployed by the Michigan Womyn's Music Festival, which categorically refused to let transsexual women onto the land, was widely repudiated by feminists who stood in solidarity with the many trans\* activist groups that led a controversial boycott of the festival.

Despite the inconsistent focus and minoritarian support of anti-transsexual feminism, the opposition between transsexual women and white feminists has emerged as a major component of contemporary transgender activism. While radical feminists such as Sheila Jeffreys and Mary Daly did articulate antipathy toward transgender women, and in so doing negatively influenced many readers, other radical feminists from the 1970s and 1980s, like Andrea Dworkin, did not see transgender women as enemies, and they understood the category of "woman" to include transgender women and even advocated for free hormones and surgery.[2] Nonetheless, the anti-transgender voices— Raymond and Jeffreys in particular—were so strident ("all transsexuals rape women's bodies," Raymond)[3] and so inflammatory ("I suggest that transsexualism should best be seen ... as directly political, medical abuse of human rights," Jeffreys)[4] that it has been hard to overcome the damage done. This has created many problems for coalition building in the United States among and between trans* and feminist groups and has lingered in such communities as an unhealed wound.

While it has been important to confront pernicious commentaries on transgender womanhood, the extremism of these feminist voices, in a sense, drowned out trans*-positive discourses in feminist venues. It has been as if transgender women have been tuned in to transphobic feminist discourse to the exclusion of all others. (The same kinds of accusations of a historically transphobic set of practices have not been articulated in relation to gay male communities, for example.) In this chapter, I propose that we relinquish the reactive positions that anti-transgender feminism has produced and move toward an affirmative trans* gender project that builds less on antagonistic standoffs and instead favors odd and quirky theories of self, other, home, world, body, identity, touching, feeling, knowing, being, becoming, and moving. To do so is to connect with other intellectual feminist genealogies, other ways of thinking that have been blocked out by this emphasis. But first, we need to understand the conflicts between some feminists and some transgender women.

The Michigan Womyn's Music Festival took place every summer in Oceana County, Michigan, from 1976 to 2015. Music festivals played an important role in the emergence of particular genres of feminism in the 1970s and 1980s, offering a performance circuit for musicians and artists as well as a separate space for women wishing time away from a society fueled by heterosexism and misogyny. MWMF was held on land owned by a woman named Lisa Vogel; run almost entirely by volunteer labor, it was attended by up to eight thousand women at a time. Over the years, the festival hosted bands like punk queers Tribe 8, folk singers like Indigo Girls, and women's music pioneers like

Holly Near and Cris Williamson.⁵ In the late 1990s transgender groups began protesting the festival for its policy of denying admission to transwomen, and a protest camp, Camp Trans, was established outside the main festival grounds. The battles between transgender activists and the womyn who set policy for MWMF were fierce and rhetorically intense, and the fallout from these conflicts was devastating.

In general, of course, there was no reason why MWMF should deny admission to trans* women; this policy of limiting access to "womyn-born womyn" felt dated and regressive even in the late 1990s. Then again, MWMF was a not-for-profit operation far outside the mainstream of American life, and it may not have been the best target for the boycott that eventually emerged. Transgender men and women in the United States in the 1990s faced discrimination in schools, at work, and in public spaces, and one could argue that these spaces, along with religious and conservative organizations, deserve our attention much more than a feminist-led annual event might. That said, transgender women were deeply hurt by this version of transphobia on the part of an organization that should have been within their solidarity network. The protests expressed this sense of betrayal.

The confrontations between the organizers of MWMF and the trans* women who wanted to attend created an archive of resentments and broken connections, and it is this history of the festival that lingers long after the annual gatherings came to an end in 2015. Indeed, these simmering disagreements made a brief but impactful appearance in *Transparent*, in an episode titled "Man on the Land" that solidified the idea of feminists and trans* people as locked in an intractable conflict. "Man on the Land," which appears at the end of season two, finds Maura (Jeffrey Tambor), a trans* woman, at the Women's Festival—not as a woman trapped in a man's body so much as a trans* woman trapped in a womyn-born womyn's event! After arriving at the festival with good faith and good vibes along with her two (sometimes) lesbian daughters, Maura learns that the festival is only for women-born women. What follows is a fantastic sequence in which various characters discuss the pros and cons of this policy in a compact and compelling way. Finally, Maura runs away from the festival, angry and hurt by the unwelcome news that she is a trespasser, a "man on the land," and she expresses a feeling of betrayal for not being recognized as female at a place created as a retreat from conventional gender politics. As she walks off the land, however, another woman, Vicky (played by Anjelica Huston), also leaving, picks her up. The two have some chemistry and go to a motel, where they have sex.

The sex scene between Maura and Vicky is quite remarkable, and it provides a beautiful, inspired, gestural response to the crude rhetoric of womanhood that they have both rejected at the women's festival. Maura, still in a putatively male body, experiences her desire via male genitalia but is able to channel that desire through her female self. The scene, directed by Jill Soloway, attended to and captured the awkwardness of bodies, the uncertainty of desire, and the weird geometries of genital compatibility. As if to bracket the polemical discussions about whether trans* women were or were not welcome on "womyn's" land, this sex scene commits to a different model of trans* feminism altogether, one that fully embraces the kind of femininity that trans* theorist Julia Serano celebrates in *Whipping Girl: A Transsexual Woman on Sexism and the Scapegoating of Femininity* as "girl stuff" and that recognizes "girl stuff" as part and parcel of complex configurations of femininity that play out across a range of bodies.[6] What makes Maura and Vicky's sexual encounter so compelling within the framework of the representation of trans* feminism and trans* femininities is the explosive energy that these two very different women's bodies are able to conjure and direct between them without either reverting to conventional male or female, masculine or feminine, positions.

Between them, Maura and her partner are an array of embodiments and identifications. They must improvise the meaning of sex and in the process find a new arrangement of desire altogether. Maura and Vicky literally recreate between them the meaning of womanhood, the meaning of lesbian, trans*, *and* heterosexual desire, and they show the foolishness of the MWMF's politics even as they reconcile to their exile from womyn-only space.

By making lemonade out of lemons, *Transparent* offers an ecstatic response to the seemingly unwavering standoff between female-born women and trans* women. The show also serves as a contemporary commentary on long-standing battles over the meaning and limits of womanhood. However, there is a danger of simplifying and reifying the multiple strands of feminist conversations over the meaning of transgender, transsexual, and trans* femininities when we focus only on the Michigan Women's Music Festival. For example, if we turn to the archive of 1970s and 1980s womyn's magazines for more concrete information on what feminists might have felt about transgender people a few decades ago, we find some surprising materials. Writings on transsexuality in feminist journals from those years yield alternative narratives about the relations between feminists and trans* people at the time.

As many trans* women have argued, some feminist groups in the 1970s and 1980s challenged transsexual women and accused them of infiltrating women-only spaces. Sandy Stone, the influential trans* theorist, for example, a member of the Olivia

Records collective, was forced out of the collective not by her lesbian feminist sisters in the group but by Janice Raymond's attacks on her and the record company and an accompanying threat of a boycott. But even in this incident we can see multiple narratives play out: even though the members of the collective disagreed with Raymond's charge that Stone was an infiltrator, obviously a small, independent label could not withstand a boycott, so they mutually agreed that Stone would leave.

There were multiple feminist positions in this standoff. While some feminists accused trans* women of trying to take over women-born women's projects, others accused trans* men of betraying women's causes and becoming the enemy when they turned male. This was the storyline in Leslie Feinberg's classic novel/memoir *Stone Butch Blues.*[7] The mutual mistrust between some feminists and some trans* people obviously has a clear history and is well documented. But it is not the whole story. Needless to say, even in this same period when feminists were refusing to admit transsexual men and women into their spaces, there were articles grappling with the meaning of transgenderism in feminist journals and magazines and zines. In a quick survey of commentary on trans* topics in some of the feminist zines and publications gathered in the One Institute Archives in Los Angeles, for example, I found a whole issue of a journal dedicated to trans* experiences, which I examine here—and it was by no means the only one.

In the Brooklyn-based journal *Echo of Sappho,* issue of summer/ fall 1973 (no. 5), we find several articles on gender transition, including a letter from someone who identified himself as a "female to male transsexual" and who suggested that the magazine "leans a little too hard on men." Elsewhere in the issue there are articles on celibacy, on BDSM, and a piece titled "The

Nature and Treatment of Transsexualism: When a Woman Becomes a Man" by one Mike Curie. This piece discusses the privileges and advantages of becoming a man but concludes: "I enjoy my status as a male, yet I realize that I don't have to prove my maleness by getting laid by women. I consider women my equals and hope to become a man who does not oppress them."[8] On the next page begins an article titled "WHY WOMEN WANT TO BECOME MEN_____AND ONE WHO DID_____!!!!" In this piece, the author explains how he got a mastectomy, the troubles he had getting a legal name change, his experience with a hysterectomy and hormones, and his near-death experience in the hospital over the course of his operations. The author was poorly treated in the hospital and emerged at the end of his ordeal with an unsuccessful bottom surgery. This author distinguishes between himself and lesbians as follows: "A lesbian is a woman who is pleased to be female and who's [sic] love object is female. A Transsexual loves females but feels trapped in the female body of her own."[9] This author clearly expected to find a sympathetic and interested audience in this magazine, and the magazine devotes considerable space to the story.

Subsequently, we find a historic essay by transgender activist Virginia Prince, who had been working with Dr. Harry Benjamin for fifteen years. She reported that while Benjamin had begun his practice with fifty-four patients a few years before, he now had a thousand patients. Both Prince and Benjamin discuss funding sex reassignment surgeries through Medicaid, and Benjamin cautions against irreversible changes and stresses that "no man is 100% man and no woman is 100% woman."[10] A final article in this issue of *Echo of Sappho* is written by a female-to-male transsexual about to go through sex reassignment surgery.

This extraordinary collection of essays, opinion pieces, and letters was not the only instance of a wide-ranging conversation in the 1970s about the newly public phenomenon of transsexuality. Rather then presenting a uniform position of feminist transphobia, the articles remind us that transsexuality was debated, scrutinized, discussed, and accepted and rejected by different feminists at different times. And while white academic feminist discourse by Janice Raymond, Sheila Jeffreys, and others seemed committed to combating transsexuals and keeping transsexuals out of "women's spaces," other venues treated trans* people as a permanent presence within women's communities. The existence of these kinds of articles challenges the prevailing notion in discussions of an anti-transgender feminism that takes the positions of one small group of influential women and makes them representative of all feminist discourse of the 1970s and 1980s. Of course, charges of transphobia among feminists are not confined to the distant past—in a contemporary context, many transgender feminists and academics continue to feel ignored or overtly critiqued by some feminist scholars who refuse to seriously engage the body of work that has now emerged under the heading of "transfeminism."

Conflicts have continued to emerge between feminists and transgender men and women, with the feminists arguing all too often that transgenderism is a capitulation to gender binarism. At the Frameline LGBT film festival in 2007, for example, a controversy broke out over a short feature by director Catherine Crouch called *The Gendercator.* Crouch described the film, a dystopian fantasy, on her website as "a short satirical take on female body modification and gender. The story uses the 'Rip van Winkle' model to extrapolate from the past into a possible future." Unfortunately, Crouch merged two distinct issues around body

modification—plastic surgery and sex reassignment surgeries—
in her nightmare vision of a gender-normative future. She noted
by way of explanation, "Things are getting very strange for
women these days. More and more often we see young heterosexual women carving their bodies into porno Barbie dolls and
lesbian women altering themselves into transmen. Our distorted
cultural norms are making women feel compelled to use medical advances to change themselves, instead of working to change
the world. This is one story, showing one possible scary future. I
am hopeful that this story will foster discussion about female
body modification and medical ethics." She also commented on
her website that the film was supposed to be satirical, imagining
as it does a world where "sex roles and gender expression are
rigidly binary and enforced by law and social custom ... one
where butch women and sissy boys are no longer tolerated—
gender variants are allowed to choose their gender, but they
must choose one and follow its rigid constraints."[11]

Crouch hoped that *The Gendercator* would provoke discussion,
and so it did, but probably not in the way she imagined. Blogs
and chat sites quickly expressed dismay that LGBT film festivals would program such a transphobic film. Frameline finally
canceled its screening in response to a petition signed by 150
people calling for the film's removal from the program. Transgender historian Susan Stryker explained on a public blog why
she had signed the petition: "I decided to support this petition
because Frameline, as an LGBT inclusive organization, is not
the appropriate venue for this sort of work. The film expresses a
long-familiar anti-transgender polemic: the idea that transsexuals are anti-gay, anti-feminist political reactionaries who col-
lude with repressive social and cultural power; furthermore,
that transsexuals are complicit in the non-consensual bodily

violation of women."[12] Stryker went on to refer to a history of anti-transgender feminism and to the problem of projecting dangerous desires onto an "alien other" and then casting that other as a threat to "our" way of life. In this case, Crouch made transsexuality complicit with a program of gender conformity (which in her film is promoted by Christian fundamentalists as well as transsexuals) and cast the gender-variant subject as a victim of new medical technologies within which the body always has a gender, one that must always be clearly expressed.

The *Gendercator* controversy, though short-lived, revealed the continuing confusion about transsexuality in terms of gender norms, victimization, other forms of body modification, cosmetic surgery, marginalization, gender transgression, and so on. The debates around the film also revealed how important it is to keep complex, theoretical discussions about gender circulating in queer communities, given the propensity for discussions to fall quickly into for-or-against modes of argumentation. The impulse to tag various media as trans-friendly or trans-phobic also shuts down the possibility of more nuanced discussion, within which one might express uncertainty about, say, the meaning of a particular mode of embodiment or concern about the circulation of hormonal therapies, without being labeled "transphobic." And finally, the castigation of one short film as the site of pernicious transphobia might overlook other problems in the film, namely the way it subscribes to a kind of consumer-oriented understanding of identity (one shared, by the way, by countless films in LGBT festivals) as something that one should be able to freely choose and cultivate, and of gender as a set of free-floating custom options for embodiment that must be protected and not submitted to a regime of forced decision making.

New discussions under the heading of "transfeminism" have begun to remedy some of these disconnects between feminists and transfeminists. In *Whipping Girl*, for example, Julia Serano reminds us that any new take on feminism must be capacious enough to include, recognize, and celebrate the femininities of women who were not born female. Not only that, but the often precarious femininity of trans* women should be seen as the centerpiece of new feminisms and not as a negation of feminist politics. Serano writes: "Until feminists work to empower femininity and pry it away from the insipid, inferior meanings that plague it—weakness, helplessness, fragility, passivity, frivolity, and artificiality—those meanings will continue to haunt every person who is female and/or feminine." Recognizing that femininity is coconstructed and coinhabited across bodies that are male and female, trans* and cis, Serano calls not just for an inclusive trans* feminism but one that actively embraces femininity rather than leaving the concept stranded in lexicons for weakness, dependence, and fear:

> We must rightly recognize that feminine expression is strong, daring, and brave—that it is powerful—and not in an enchanting, enticing, or supernatural sort of way, but in a tangible, practical way that facilitates openness, creativity, and honest expression. We must move beyond seeing femininity as helpless and dependent, or merely as masculinity's sidekick, and instead acknowledge that feminine expression exists of its own accord and brings its own rewards to those who naturally gravitate toward it. By embracing femininity, feminism will finally be able to reach out to the vast majority of feminine women who have felt alienated by the movement in the past.[13]

Serano's work is important because it recognizes how feminism has managed to be *about* women and has worked hard to expose gender hierarchies, but has done so without reinvesting in femininity in the process. Indeed, many versions of feminisms have viewed femininity with suspicion, characterizing it as pure artifice, as theater and as performance. Serano, however, like many trans* theorists, resists this notion of femininity, and gender in general, as a performance ("If one more person tells me that 'all gender is performance,' I think I am going to strangle them").[14] Although she recognizes that trans*women cocreate femininities with cisgender women, Serano and others worry that adopting performativity as a theoretical rubric implies, in a transphobic way, that trans* gender is not real, material, authentic. Yet this resistance to the notion of gender performance as a concept has set up another site of antagonism that operates alongside the radical versus trans* feminism divide—namely, queer theory versus trans theory. In the early days of trans* theory, some of this antagonism was directed at the work of philosopher Judith Butler (who will be discussed in greater depth below).

Transgender/transsexual objections to Butler's work have arisen from a recommitment to essentialism within transsexual theory—Jay Prosser, Vi Namaste, Henry Rubin, Stephen Whittle, and others, at various times, have read the emphasis in poststructuralist gender theories on performativity as a way of denying the need for some trans* people to undergo sex reassignment surgeries.[15] The most complex articulation of transsexual suspicion of Butlerian gender theory occurred in Jay Prosser's 1998 book *Second Skins: Body Narratives of Transsexuality*, a classic early text on male transgender narratives. Prosser asked what effect a theory of gender performativity had had on an emergent understandings of transsexuality; he also argued that for all our talk about "materiality" and "embodiment," it is precisely the body that vanishes within ever more abstract theories of gender, sexuality, and desire. Prosser commented specifically on the close relationship between queerness and gender performativity and situated transsexuality as a nonperformative relation to materiality. He also took issue with the way the trans* body came to stand in for bodily plasticity in many poststructuralist discussions of gender. He wrote: "Queer's alignment of itself with transgender performativity represents queer's sense of its own 'higher purpose,' in fact there are transgendered trajectories, in particular transsexual trajectories, that aspire to that which this scheme devalues. Namely, there are transsexuals who seek very pointedly to be nonperformative, to be constative, quite simply, to be."[16]

Prosser's work was enormously influential, for it articulated in a gloriously complex way many of the misgivings that transgender theorists felt about queer conjurings of gender flexibility, gender plasticity, and gender performance. This emphasis on the real for trans* people was a valuable intervention in the late 1990s, coming at a time when transgender people were often viewed within medicine and psychology as delusional, pathological, and dangerously dysphoric. More recently, however, trans* theory has swung back around to these oppositions between realness and performance, and, as we have seen in the work of J. R. Latham and Micha Cárdenas, new understandings of "transrealities" have emerged alongside deep engagement with the notion of performance and performativity.[17] The tension that seemed to animate Prosser's early critiques of Butler have now been dispelled within the discourses of trans* feminism, which borrow from early trans* narratives and Butlerian gender theory alike.

Poststructuralist theory, indeed, mostly offered theorizations of gender that deny the anchoring of social identity to some concretely and immutably gendered body. Judith Butler's concept of "gender performativity," despite becoming the target of so many trans* critiques, actually furnished trans* theorists with the theoretical framings necessary to push back on essentialist accounts of normative identities, on the one hand, and the fetishizing gaze at transgender bodies, on the other. Butler's extensive work on gender and sexuality has been generative within queer and trans* and feminist circles partly because in it we find not only the principles that have created deep divisions but also the seeds of rapprochement. Indeed, tensions over Butler's legacy in relation to the vexed topic of "gender transgression" illuminate just how confused feminist discourse can be about the meaning of gender fixity and gender flexibility and the relation of each to normativity and transgression.

For some, gender fixity is a sign of the stubbornness of identification (Lisa Diamond, for example, favors the idea of "sexual fluidity"),[18] and for others gender flexibility is the indication that discourse has its limits and that some basic human instinct for variation always escapes gender ideologies. The work of Judith Butler that has been so influential within both feminism and trans* theory advances the idea that all bodies must submit to gender norms but that some bodies can repeat those norms to the point of absurdity, shaking loose from some of the confinement that those norms enact. In *Gender Trouble* in 1990, Butler rewrote liberal feminism and even parts of Western philosophy by making the gender-variant woman the subject of each.[19] While the masculine woman, she claimed, was unthinkable within French feminism because of its commitment to a gender-stable and unified conception of womanhood, masculinity was similarly unthinkable as female for continental philosophy and for psychoanalysis. In *Gender Trouble,* rather, gender was a site of constraint not flexibility. In the book that followed in 1993, *Bodies That Matter,* Butler responded to various misreadings of her earlier work, precisely around the topic of flexibility, and attempted again to emphasize the inflexibility of the gendered condition, its resistance to voluntary action, and its availability for only discrete re-significations.[20] While in *Gender Trouble* the butch body made mischievous trouble for all stable understandings of the category "woman," *Bodies That Matter* deployed that body to make trouble for all stable understandings of masculine power (the phallus) that could not conceive of masculinity without men. In neither book, however, was gender flexible; rather, it was the inflexibility of a female commitment to masculinity in each case that signified the thorn in the side of feminism and psychoanalytic conceptions of the phallus. Finally, in *Undoing Gender* (2004) Butler returned to the entwined interests of transgenderism, intersexuality, and transsexuality to argue that gender stability plays a crucial role in the production of the category of the "human." Indeed, many of our understandings of the human proceed from and presume gender normativity as a foundation for other modes of being. In this book she calls for "recognition" for trans modes of being.

Despite her rigorous critique of foundationalist notions of the gendered body, Butler has sometimes been positioned as a queer feminist with questionable views on trans politics. In *Undoing Gender,* Butler goes to great lengths to dispel this particular characterization of her work, and she places gender transitivity at the very heart of political life: "The suggestions that butch, femme, and transgendered lives are not essential referents for a refashioning of political life, and for a more just and equitable society, fails to acknowledge the violence that the otherwise gendered suffer in the public world and fails as well to recognize that embodiment denotes a contested set of norms governing who will count as a viable subject within the sphere of politics."[21]

As we approach the third decade of the twenty-first century, the standoff between radical feminism and trans* feminism continues to be represented as a live and urgent issue. In May 2016 the *Transgender Studies Quarterly*, in an issue dedicated to "Trans/ Feminisms," featured an introductory essay by Paisley Currah in which Currah suggests that despite many shifts and changes, feminist positions still coincide too often with transphobic rhetoric. "The persistence of limited but recurring outbursts of feminist transphobia," he warns, "cannot be explained away simply as a displacement of a more generalized generational antipathy between the second and third waves of feminism. Nor is it useful to dismiss these outbursts as minor atavistic eruptions in the greater march toward gender equality."[22] Currah usefully reminds his readers that the opposition between trans and cisgendered bodies is losing traction in newly expansive definitions of gender transitivity. The special issue of the journal, he notes, attends to the much-traversed boundary between trans and feminist even as it continues to track conflict and suspicion between the two.

The "Trans/Feminisms" issue of *TSQ* includes a second introductory essay by managing editor Susan Stryker and long-time transgender scholar and activist Talia M. Bettcher. In this piece, Stryker and Bettcher express dismay about new forms of "anti-transgender backlash" in feminist circles, citing a book by Sheila Jeffreys and a few articles about Caitlin Jenner in support of their claim that we are witnessing "an escalating struggle over public speech."[23] Ultimately, however, and to their credit, Stryker and Bettcher are more interested in outlining a trans* feminism that has emerged from within transgender movements themselves than in continuing to invest in a potentially counterproductive argument with feminists like Jeffreys, who prove to be unrepresentative of new generations of feminist thought and out of touch with activist contexts.

Stryker and Bettcher instead try to shift the conversation away from transphobic feminism, citing from other feminist traditions of thought in order to find fruitful connections between different strands of struggle for gender justice. They note, for example, the importance of Kimberle Crenshaw's notion of intersectionality to an emergent trans/feminist position,[24] and they mention the biographies of several trans men and trans women of color who represent very different trajectories of gender nonconformity than the standoff between white transgender women and white feminists might imply. Stryker and Bettcher turn also to the life of transwoman and Stonewall Riots leader Sylvia Rivera as evidence of an articulation of feminist principles from within a burgeoning transgender liberation movement.

> In 1973, when Sylvia Rivera—Stonewall veteran and cofounder of the Street Transvestite Action Revolutionaries (STAR)—fought her way onto the stage of the Christopher Street Liberation Day rally in New York, after having first been blocked by antitrans lesbian feminists and their gay male supporters, she spoke defiantly of her own experiences of being raped and beaten by predatory heterosexual men she had been incarcerated with, and of the work that she and others in STAR were doing to support other incarcerated trans women. She chastised the crowd for not being more supportive of trans people who experienced exactly the sort of gendered violence that feminists typically decried and asserted, with her own characteristic brio, that "the women who have tried to fight for their sex changes, or to become women, are the women's liberation."[25]

This is a great quote from Rivera, and as Stryker and Bettcher astutely note, Rivera articulates a truly liberatory vision of womanhood, one around which, moreover, multiple feminist agendas could coalesce absent the seemingly inevitable standoff between lesbian feminists and those could-be and would-be trans* allies. Trans* feminist filmmaker Reina Gossett has recently begun to document and narrate the lives and struggles of trans* activists of color such as Marsha P. Johnson and Sylvia Rivera, and undoubtedly her new film and other work like this will change the stories we tell about trans* feminism.

In this chapter, I have tried to suggest that the vexed relations between transgender activism and theory, on the one hand, and feminist activism and theory, on the other, are a real problem for contemporary political alliances. The opportunity that faces contemporary trans* theory is to reset the terms of these debates: rather than remaining invested in an identitarian set of conflicts that turn on small differences and individual hurts, let us rather wage battle against the violent imposition of economic disparity and forcefully oppose a renewed and open investment in white supremacy and American imperial ambition transacted through the channels of globalization. Notably, trans* feminisms in other places, like Latin America, are less likely to culminate in such standoffs. Claudia Sofía Garriga-López, for example, has written at length about transfeminism in Ecuador, which she describes as "a grassroots political project rooted in material politics" that understands transgender liberation as central to the fight against patriarchal systems. This particular version of feminism, Garriga-López shows, recognizes sites of shared struggle between trans sex workers, home makers, gang members, punk rockers, and others who share what she calls "subjacent symmetries."[26]

In an article titled "Transfeminist Crossroads," Garriga-López tells the story of the compromises and conflicts, the shared visions and divided loyalties, that beset a transfeminist activist group in Ecuador that tried to get a bill passed allowing people to list their gender and not their birth sex on their identification papers. This struggle did not conclude with the desired outcome, however: although trans* people won the right to change their sex and get a special "alternative ID," the group did not manage to persuade the legislature that the shift should be universal, applicable to all people. Nonetheless, Garriga-López draws hope from the grassroots movement and uses it to show that "transfeminism is not a one-way flow of solidarity from nontrans feminists toward trans people" but instead that "trans activists have been at the forefront of feminist and LGBT struggles for many decades, and the category of 'transfeminism' signals the articulation of these practices into a cohesive political standpoint."[27] This point is crucial in any quest to move forward toward multiple visions of trans* futurity and away from the traps of internecine conflict; in other words, feminism has always been articulated by trans* activists and trans* activism has always been feminist. Garriga-López's research beautifully broadens the scope of the conversation and reminds us of how narrow the landscapes of the United States and Europe are relative to more global understandings of the politics of trans*.

The hostile and intractable conflicts that have marked struggles over the meaning of womanhood can also be challenged by using new models of embodiment and identity. As I have highlighted in this book, work on the haptic and the fractal (Vacarro), the architectural (Crawford), and the somatic (Hayward) pushes away from idealized notions of discrete bodies laying claim to well-established categories of *male* and *female*. These new theoretical portals offer a different language for embodiment that draws from human-animal relations, uncertain experiences of embodiment, and haphazard, profuse, and viral models of embodiment. In her beautiful essay "Spider City Sex," for example, Eva Hayward uses the concept of neighborhood rather than home to elaborate a theory of transition. "What," she asks, "is the somatic sociality of trans-becoming?"[28] This is a massive improvement on questions like "Who is a woman?" or "What is womanhood?" or even "What are the relations between trans* and cis-womanhood?" because it recognizes the way that categories of being emerge alongside each other as part of what Garriga-López calls "subjacent symmetries," as a relation to environment, habitat, buildings, and the other creatures who share those spaces with us. Hayward, for example, asks about the relations between transitioning women and spiders! Spiders, she offers, "are their own architects, creating resonating places that are home and territory."[29] The webbing and weaving in which the spiders engage offer a beautiful and compelling model for the transitions and space-making creativity of a trans* feminism that cuts loose from unproductive antagonisms and thinks with nonhuman beings about how to make a world.

In the new landscapes of power and domination that emerge at the beginning of a potentially disastrous shift from neoliberal mechanics of inclusion to the postdemocratic policies of violent exclusion and the enforcement of homogeneity, we need to situate sexual and gender minorities carefully rather than claiming any predetermined status of precarity or power. It remains to be seen what the enemy will do, but one thing is sure, for trans* people everywhere, the true enemy has nothing to do with feminism.

# Conclusions

## *Making and Un-Making Bodies*

Play well *(leg godt)*.[1]

Transgender and transsexuality may even be
exemplary architectural practices and also the very
bases for thinking of bodies architecturally.
Lucas Crawford, "Breaking Ground on a
Theory of Transgender Architecture" (2010)

Moving forward, then, or onward, or outward, I offer a final
framework, culled from the exciting and counterintuitive work
on trans* embodiment that I have commented on and dialogued
with in this book, in the hopes of pushing us in different directions for future considerations of gender variability, social
change, and new political formations. I propose to use this frame
to rethink the meaning of identity, body, politics, and movement. The terminology I offer may strike some people as odd or
whimsical, silly, or even offensive; it is not intended to give
offense, but it is certainly well within the bounds of the nonseri-
ous. My terminology comes from Lego and uses the moveable
parts and freestyle building processes associated with Lego to

think seriously about new bodily architectures, component parts of embodiment, and structures of becoming.

✦  ✦  ✦

Lego, the brightly colored, irresistible building blocks that kids use to create whole worlds, has its own language; one cheery website even invites readers to "learn to speak Lego."[2] It turns out there are some pretty useful terms: individual Lego pieces are called "elements," for example, or "bricks," which are further differentiated into studs, anti-studs, tiles, stamps, plates, et cetera. People who play with Legos, adult or child, are called "builders," and a creation built without instructions is a MOC (My Own Creation). A "Rainbow Warrior," we learn, is any multicolored creation that a beginner might build. Lego worlds arise from multiplying "vignettes" and "bignettes"—the bignette being a larger version of the vignette (a small scene, typically built on a base 8 studs long by 8 studs wide).[3]

The idea of using Lego language to think through future forms of life and living spaces was put to good use in *The Lego Movie* (2014, dir. Phil Lord and Chris Miller). The film introduces us to a world of improvised and endlessly shifting built environments that are dreamed up by architects, built by master builders, and inhabited by Lego people, block figures who can, presumably, also shift the geometries of their bodies. This utopian world comes under threat from a corporate figure, Lord Business, who tries to reduce the unruliness of this social order and limit its variability, its chaotic nature, and its unpredictability. Indeed, he moves against the improvisational quality of Lego worlds, which can be built and unbuilt at will, with a tube of superglue, threatening to fix the disaggregated nature of Lego people once and for all. Lord Business also deploys a combination of positive thinking with nonstop commercialization (whose theme song is "Everything Is Awesome") in order to dull his people into submission. In *The Lego Movie*, as in almost no contemporary films aimed at audiences over the age of eighteen, the citizens of Legoburg rise up and fight for their right to reimagine their world. The frame of the film involves a struggle between a father and children who are playing with Legos—the father wants to use the Legos to build a recognizable world, a version of the one he already inhabits, while his children want to freestyle and make something wholly different, a place that is unrecognizable within the current rules of architecture, order, beauty, and symmetry.

Many of the themes of this book can be found, oddly (or not), in *The Lego Movie*. I have argued along with Lucas Crawford for thinking with the architectural terms we use to describe the body (home, temple, frame); I am taken with the idea that, as Crawford puts it, "transgender and transsexuality may even be exemplary architectural practices."[4] Noting that architectures both mimic and produce bodies, and that bodies influence and inhabit architecture, Crawford goes one step further and looks at the way an architectural logic informs our understanding of the body. When we think of our body as a home, a common trope in transgender biographies, we commit ourselves to all kinds of normative inscriptions of embodiment: the domestic, ownership, and fixity come to mind. If we shift our focus, as Crawford proposes, away from the housing of the body and toward the notion of "transition"—perpetual transition—we can commit to a horizon of possibility where the future is not male or female but transgender.

Lego architectures are in a constant state of emergence and collapse. The child brings home their new Lego set with its tidy packages of pieces and its orderly instructions for assembly and after a few days of building according to the instructions they knock the whole thing down and start again, making smaller or larger, simpler or more complex environments, improvising structures and learning the functions of walls and doors, the excitement of balancing mobility against grandeur, the humility of creating systems that do not work or vehicles that do not move or leaky architectures or flightless planes. The world of Lego is one of constant transition, and while there is always the possibility of returning to the instruction sheet and following the step-by-step directions, the uncharted territory of creation always beckons. Until very recently, Lego environments lacked humanoid figures allowing the child builders to understand themselves as the inhabitants of the worlds they built. But in the 1970s Lego introduced "minifigures," a series of humanlike characters that can also be assembled out of moveable parts. Early on these minifigs, as they are called, were all yellow and featured smiley faces. Newer versions come in different colors and have different facial expressions and features. Minifigs appealed to children but did not replace the overall charm of building cities, machines, and social worlds.

In *The Lego Movie,* the protagonists, minifigs themselves, hunt for a fabled "piece of resistance," the only Lego piece that can stop Lord Business from gluing the world into the shape that most benefits him. This lovely notion of a literal "piece of resistance" might also stand as a metaphor for the force of trans* re-creation. The glued and stuck world that Lord Business desires fails to materialize when Lord Business is confronted with the piece—the piece, not surprisingly perhaps, is a cap for the superglue weapon that Lord Business seeks to unleash upon the restless world under his command. This piece—part phallus, part vessel—prevents the flow of glue and protects the world of components from becoming a concrete land of fixity and stasis.

The importance of the architectural paradigm will be lost on no one who has visited a public restroom recently. Such venues have become the sites of intense struggle recently in relation to the presumption that all bodies fall into one of two categories and that these two categories, male and female, are all that are needed to neatly divide up the spaces where people choose to relieve themselves when away from home. Some twenty years ago, in my second book, *Female Masculinity,* I wrote about something I called "the bathroom problem." Noting the tendency for women to police each other in the women's bathroom and for men to cruise each other, I tried to investigate the protocols of gender scrutiny as they play out every day in public restrooms across the country and even around the world. The bathroom, I claimed then, is a technology of gender, a mode of sorting, producing, and sustaining gender norms in a public sphere where those same norms were rapidly disintegrating. And so, even back in the mid-1990s, long before the bathroom battles that emerged in the middle of the 2016 election season, the question of bathroom etiquette vexed and bothered both cis- and trans gender-identified bodies. The sorting of bodies through seemingly irrefutable, inevitable, and obvious signage masked the intense enforcement of a set of gender norms through mechanisms that were cleverly folded into quotidian divisions of space. The bathroom, I claimed then, and I continue to claim now, represents the breakdown of a system that over time and across multiple geographies has accrued a patina of permanence and stability. As the cracks begin to show under the pressure exerted by the public emergence of trans* bodies and a widespread dissatisfaction with the policing of space, we are now regaled with a series of laws—and opposition to them—designed to give trans* people harassment-free access to public facilities.

The bathroom battles this time around began in 2015 with a series of "bathroom bills" giving trans* people access to bathrooms that match their gender rather than their sex as assigned at birth. These bills were based on nondiscrimination ordinances and responded to the increasing numbers of gender-non-conforming bodies in public spaces and the ensuing battles for space, access, and mobility. Like gay marriage before it, the bathroom in American life has provided a testing ground for social theories of difference.[5] While marriage laws in the United States have provided the bedrock for white supremacy by legally prohibiting or permitting interracial unions, so bathroom bills have formed one historical track within the control of space and the legally mandated and enforced divisions between white and black bodies in this country in the years following the end of slavery. The bathroom bills, indeed, should be seen as part of what some scholars call "the afterlife of slavery," a period within which legacies of slavery linger and form the basis for new understandings of bondage and freedom.

The bathroom problem can be situated within this emergent architectural paradigm for trans* studies. Rather than seeking to grant or deny access, then, we should be rethinking the function, the purpose, and the productive force of the architectures we inhabit and the architectural logic we use when we "assume a body," to quote Gayle Salomon.[6] Like so many features of mainstream political discourse, the bathroom problem fixates on one site of contestation and proposes that a resolution in that site will be a resolution in every site. But we know this is false. The bathroom problem is a symptom and not a cause of current disputes about the body, and as such we cannot resolve a solution to this problem without unlocking new understandings of public space, intimate acts, and personal care of the body. Why not ask architectural questions about what bathrooms could be rather than call on architecture to simply fix gender ideologies that dictate separate bathrooms for male-ish and female-ish bodies? Once we have reorganized our sense of bodily difference, we will, I propose, find our way to new ways to house them, to open them up to change, and to enclose and sequester them. Just as gay marriage was never the right solution to correcting the problems of the institution of marriage, with its exclusionary and regulatory mechanisms, so transgender bathrooms will not be the solution to the problems with gender-segregated bathrooms, locker rooms, clubs, lounges, gyms, and schools.

Indeed, resolutions to seemingly intractable issues involving gender and sexual difference should in general feature a fix that is for everyone rather than merely an extension of rights to the aggrieved population. As Stefano Harney and Fred Moten propose in their brilliant book *The Undercommons,* the way to address persistent problems of racism, sexism, and homophobia is to see that discrimination does not only impact the people toward whom it is directed, it affects everyone. Harney and Moten write of a coalition of interests—not an interest group or even an interested group, but a coalition—that understands that change for some means change for everyone: "The coalition emerges out of your recognition that it's fucked up for you, in the same way that we've already recognized that it's fucked up for us. I don't need your help. I just need you to recognize that this shit is killing you, too, however much more softly, you stupid motherfucker, you know?"[7]

Trans* bodies, in their fragmented, unfinished, broken-beyond-repair forms, remind all of us that the body is always under construction. Whether trans* bodies are policed in bathrooms or seen as killers and loners, as thwarted, lonely, violent, or tormented, they are also a site for invention, imagination, fabulous projection. Trans* bodies represent the art of becoming, the necessity of imagining, and the fleshly insistence of transitivity.

# ACKNOWLEDGMENTS

This book owes a very large debt to the four anonymous trans* studies readers who gave generous and hard-hitting feedback at several stages. The book not only is better for their input, but it hopefully sidesteps all kinds of problems that were present in the first iterations of the manuscript. One of these problems concerns the lopsided representations of trans*men and trans*women in the book. This book still skews toward trans* masculinity, and I have in no way corrected the imbalance, but I have learned much from the many writings of trans* women to which I have been introduced in the course of my recent research. The emphasis on trans* masculinity here is also not simply the continued privileging of masculine experiences of embodiment over feminine experiences; it also hopefully errs on the side of correcting earlier theories and narratives of trans* life that were wholly based on material gathered from trans* feminine subjects.

I also received generous and skillful editorial guidance from Lisa Duggan. I thank her profusely for her insight and intelligence and for creating this remarkable series of public intellectual interventions into current events and topics. I thank her as well for her sustained friendship and support. Other thanks go to colleagues in the field of trans* studies, some of whom I may not know personally but from all of whom I have learned much: Aren Aizura, Lucas Crawford, Eva Hayward, Joe Latham, Gayle Salamon, Susan Stryker, and Jeanne Vacarro. And further thanks are due to my bullyblogger comrades, Lisa Duggan, Eng Beng Lim, Tavia Nyong'o, and José Quiroga. Finally, credit to trans* and queer kin who have influenced my work with theirs: boychild, Ceci Bastida, Jayna Brown, Judith Butler, Sara Davidmann, Harry Dodge, Rod Ferguson, Chandra Ford, Gayatri Gopinath, Stefano Harney, Silas Howard, Kara Keeling, Josh Kun, Ira Livingston, Lisa Lowe, Iona Mancheong, Kim Peirce, Fred Moten, Maggie Nelson, Chandan Reddy, Riley Snorton, Wu Tsang. A special mention for María Elena Martínez, whose work I use quite a bit in this book and who died way too young and with so much more to teach us. Thank you to Mena Tajrishi for research assistance. And a big shout out to all my new colleagues at Columbia University. Trans* love and admiration always to Macarena Gomez-Barris and her mini-me's.

# NOTES

## PREFACE

1. Daniel Kreps, "Prince Warns Young Artists: Record Contracts Are 'Slavery,'" *Rolling Stone,* August 9, 2015, www.rollingstone.com /music/news/prince-warns-young-artists-record-contracts-are-slavery-20150809.

## CHAPTER ONE. TRANS*

1. Herman Melville, *Moby Dick* (1851; London: Constable & Co., 1922).

2. Charles Dickens, *Great Expectations* (1860; Peterborough, Ont.: Broadview Press, 1998).

3. Franz Kafka, *The Metamorphosis,* edited by Stanley Corngold (1915; Toronto: Bantam Books, 1981).

4. Salman Rushdie, *Midnight's Children* (1981; New York: Random House, 2006).

5. Respectively, Ralph Ellison, *Invisible Man* (New York: Random House, 1952); and Samuel Beckett, *The Unnamable* (1953; New York: Faber and Faber, 2009).

6. *Finding Nemo,* dir. Andrew Stanton (Buena Vista Pictures, 2003).

7. Many trans scholars, including Susan Stryker, have weighed in on the term "trans\*," and while some trans people resist its ambiguity, the critical discourse on the use of "trans\*" has been mostly affirmative.

8. Joanne Meyerowitz, "America's Original Transgender Sweetheart," *Politico Magazine,* June 16, 2015, www.politico.com/magazine/story/2015/06/caitlyn-jenner-was-not-americas-first-transgender-sweetheart-christine-jorgensen-119080. Christine Jorgensen was quoted as saying, "Just how does a child tell its parents such a story as this … I am still the same old Brud (nickname), but my dears, nature made a mistake which I have corrected and now I am your daughter" (Ben White, "Ex-GI Becomes Blonde Beauty: Operations Transform Bronx Youth," *New York Daily News,* December 1, 1952, www.nydailynews.com/new-york/bronx-army-vet-ground-breaking-sex-change-1952-article-1.2198836).

9. Radclyffe Hall, *The Well of Loneliness* (Garden City, NY: Sun Dial Press, 1928).

10. See Fredrick Winslow Taylor, *The Principles of Scientific Management* (New York: Harper & Bros., 1911).

11. Cesare Lombroso and William Ferrero, *The Female Offender* (New York: D. Appleton & Co., 1989).

12. Richard Krafft-Ebing, *Psychopathia Sexualis, with Special Reference to Contrary Sexual Instinct: A Medico-Legal Study* (Philadelphia: F. A. Davis Co., 1886).

13. Michel Foucault, *History of Sexuality,* vol. 1: *An Introduction,* translated by Robert Hurley (New York: Random House, 1978).

14. Maggie Nelson, *The Argonauts* (Minneapolis: Graywolf Press, 2015), 8.

15. Ariel Levy, "Dolls and Feelings," *New Yorker,* December 14, 2015, www.newyorker.com/magazine/2015/12/14/dolls-and-feelings.

16. Ibid.

17. Dean Spade, *Normal Life: Administrative Violence, Critical Trans Politics, and the Limits of the Law* (Durham, NC: Duke University Press, 2016); Eric A. Stanley and Nat Smith, eds., *Captive Genders: Trans Embodiment and the Prison Industrial Complex,* expanded 2nd ed. (Oakland, CA: AK Press, 2015).

18. Heklina, "The Trouble With Tranny," *Studies in Gender and Sexuality* 16 (2015): 142–43.

19. L. H. Stallings, *Funk the Erotic: Transaesthetics and Black Sexual Cultures* (Champaign: University of Illinois Press, 2015), 232.

20. Ibid.

21. Ibid.

22. *Monty Python's Life of Brian*, dir. Terry Jones (Cinema International Corporation [UK], Orion Pictures/Warner Bros. [US], 1979).

23. The scene can be viewed at www.youtube.com/watch?v= IIAdHEwiAy8.

24. Andrew R. Flores, Jody L. Herman, Gary J. Gates, and Taylor N. Brown, "How Many Adults Identify as Transgender in the United States," Williams Institute, Los Angeles, 2016.

25. The Center for Disease Control reports that "transgender women are at a high risk for HIV" but also adds that "half of transgender people diagnoses with HIV are Black/African American" (www .cdc.gov/hiv/group/gender/transgender).

26. On the issue of suicide: it is hard to judge how many transgender people have attempted suicide, but the Williams Institute reports unusually high rates for transgender women in particular. See Ann P. Haas, Jody L.Herman, and Philip L. Rodgers, "Suicide Attempts among Transgender and Gender Non-Conforming Adults," Williams Institute, Los Angeles, 2014. Suicide attempts could, however, be over-reported among this population because attempted suicide is often used as a metric in psychological examinations of transgender people when doctors and therapists are assessing their suitability for surgery and prescribed hormone treatments.

27. Wynne Perry, "Gender Dysphoria: DSM-5 Reflects Shift in Perspective on Gender Identity," *Huffington Post,* June 4, 2013. www.huffing tonpost.com/2013/06/04/gender-dysphoria-dsm-5_n_3385287.html.

28. This scene can be viewed at www.youtube.com/watch?v= R79yYo2aOZs.

29. Stallings, *Funk the Erotic,* 10.

30. For "genderlessness," see Gayle Rubin, "The Traffic in Women: Notes on the 'Political Economy' of Sex" (1975), in *The Second Wave,* edited by Linda Nicholson (New York: Routledge, 1997), 27–62. The term "gender hacked" can be found in Paul B. Preciado, *Testo-Junkie: Sex, Drugs, and Biopolitics in the Pharmacopornographic Era* (New York: Feminist Press, 2013).

CHAPTER TWO. MAKING TRANS* BODIES

1. Pagan Kennedy, *The First Man-Made Man: The Story of Two Sex Changes, One Love Affair, and a Twentieth-Century Medical Revolution* (London: Bloomsbury, 2007), 60.

2. Lucas Cassidy Crawford, "Breaking Ground on a Theory of Transgender Architecture," *Seattle Journal for Social Justice* 8, no. 2 (2010): 515–39; available at http://digitalcommons.law.seattleu.edu/sjsj /vol8/iss2/5.

3. Sherry Velasco, *The Lieutenant Nun: Transgenderism, Lesbian Desire, and Catalina de Erauso* (Austin: University of Texas Press, 2000); Gary Kates, *Monsieur d'Éon Is a Woman: A Tale of Political Intrigue and Sexual Masquerade* (Baltimore: Johns Hopkins University Press, 1995).

4. María Elena Martínez, "Archives, Bodies, and Imagination: The Case of Juana Aguilar and Queer Approaches to History, Sexuality, and Politics," *Radical History Review*, no. 120 (Fall 2014): 159.

5. Ibid.

6. Michael Dillon, *Self: A Study in Endocrinlogy and Ethics* (1946; Oxford: Butterworth-Heinemann, 2013).

7. Kennedy, *First Man-Made Man*, 14.

8. For an alternative to the conventional narrative of the impossibility of bottom surgery for trans men in particular, see Trystan Cotton's valuable collection of testimonies in *Hung Jury: Testimonies of Genital Surgery by Transsexual Men* (San Francisco: Transgress Press, 2012). For an early narrative that details the pleasure and the pain of SRS for transwomen, see Claudine Griggs, *Passage to Trinidad* (1996; London: Bloomsbury Academic, 2005).

9. Scott Lauria Morgensen, *Spaces between Us: Queer Settler Colonialism and Indigenous Decolonization* (Minneapolis: University of Minnesota Press, 2011), 1.

10. See, e.g., Paul B. Preciado, *Testo Junkie: Sex, Drugs, and Biopolitics in the Pharmacopornographic Era* (2008), translated from the French by Bruce Benderson (New York: Feminist Press at the City University of New York, 2013); idem, *Pornotopia: An Essay on Playboy's Architecture and Biopolitics* (Cambridge, MA: MIT Press/Zone Books, 2014).

11. See Gilles Deleuze and Félix Guattari, *Anti-Oedipus: Capitalism and Schizophrenia,* translated by Robert Hurley, Mark Seem, and Helen R. Lane (Minneapolis: University of Minnesota Press, 1983); Sigmund Freud, *Three Essays on the Theory of Sexuality* (1905), translated by James Strachey (New York: Basic Books, 2000); and Michel Foucault, *The History of Sexuality,* vol. 1: *An Introduction,* translated by Robert Hurley (New York: Random House, 1978).

12. Maggie Nelson, *The Argonauts* (Minneapolis: Graywolf Press, 2015), 83.

13. Christoph Hanssmann, "Feminist Inquiries and Trans-Health Politics and Practices," *TSQ: Transgender Studies Quarterly* 3, nos. 1–2 (May 2016): 120–136.

14. J.R. Latham, "(Re)Making Sex: A Praxiography of the Gender Clinic," *Feminist Theory,* March 2017; available at http://journals.sagepub.com/doi/pdf/10.1177/1464700117700051. See also idem, "Trans Men's Sexual Narrative-Practices: Introducing STS to Trans and Sexuality Studies." *Sexualities* 19, no. 3 (2016): 347–68.

15. David Valentine, *Imagining Transgender: An Ethnography of a Category* (Durham, NC: Duke University Press, 2007).

16. Roderick A. Ferguson, *Aberrations in Black: Toward a Queer of Color Critique* (Minneapolis: University of Minnesota Press, 2003).

17. Riley Snorton, *Black on Both Sides: A Racial History of Trans Identity* (Minneapolis: University of Minnesota Press, 2017).

18. Hortense Spillers, "Mama's Baby, Papa's Maybe: An American Grammar Book," *Diacritics* 17, no. 2 (Summer 1987): 65–81.

19. See also Aren Z. Aizura, "The Romance of the Amazing Scalpel: 'Race,' Labour, and Affect in Thai Gender Reassignment Clinics," in *Queer Bangkok: 21st-Century Markets, Media, and Rights,* edited by Peter Jackson (Hong Kong: Hong Kong University Press, 2011), 144–62.

20. See, e.g., Dean Spade, *Normal Life: Administrative Violence, Critical Trans Politics, and the Limits of Law* (Durham, NC: Duke University Press, 2011); and Toby Beauchamp, "Artful Concealment and Strategic Visibility: Transgender Bodies and U.S. State Surveillance after 9/11," in *The Transgender Studies Reader 2,* edited by Aren Aizura and Susan Stryker (New York: Routledge, 2013), 46–55.

21. https://en.wikipedia.org/wiki/Fremde_Haut.

22. Fatima El-Tayeb, *European Others: Queering Ethnicity in Postnational Europe* (Minneapolis: University of Minnesota Press, 2011), 81–120.

23. Giorgio Agamben, *Homo Sacer: Sovereign Power and Bare Life,* translated by Daniel Heller-Roazen (Palo Alto: Stanford University Press, 1998).

24. Afsaneh Najmabadi, *Professing Selves: Transsexuality and Same-Sex Desire in Contemporary Iran (Experimental Futures)* (Durham, NC: Duke University Press, 2013), 1.

25. Ibid., 4.

## CHAPTER THREE. BECOMING TRANS*

1. *Diagnostic and Statistical Manual of Mental Disorders,* 2nd and 5th eds. (Washington, DC: American Psychiatric Association, 1968 and 2013).

2. National Center for Transgender Equality, "About Us," 2017, www.transequality.org/about.

3. Sylvia Rivera Law Project (SRLP), "About SRLP," 2017, https://srlp.org/about.

4. Dean Spade, *Normal Life: Administrative Violence, Critical Trans Politics, and the Limits of Law* (Durham, NC: Duke University Press, 2011), 13.

5. Gail Bederman, *Manliness and Civilization: A Cultural History of Gender and Race in the United States, 1880–1917* (Chicago: University of Chicago Press, 1995).

6. Sarah Haley, *No Mercy Here: Gender, Punishment, and the Making of Jim Crow Modernity* (Chapel Hill: University of North Carolina Press, 2016), 5–6. Also see Hortense J. Spillers, "Mama's Baby, Papa's Maybe: An American Grammar Book," *Diacritics* 17, no. 2 (Summer 1987): 64–81.

7. Eva Hayward and Jami Weinstein, "Introduction: Tranimalities in the Age of Trans* Life," *TSQ: Transgender Studies Quarterly* 2, no. 2 (2015): 195–208.

8. Wendy McKenna and Suzanne J. Kessler, *Gender: An Ethnomethodological Approach* (Chicago: University of Chicago Press, 1978).

9. Judith Butler, *Gender Trouble: Feminism and the Subversion of Identity* (New York: Routledge, 1990).

10. Michel Foucault, *History of Sexuality*, vol. 1: *An Introduction*, translated by Robert Hurley (New York: Random House, 1978).

11. Jasbir Puar, "Bodies with New Organs Becoming Trans, Becoming Disabled," *Social Text* 33, no. 3 (September 2015): 52.

12. Ibid., 63.

13. Kathryn Bond Stockton, *The Queer Child, or Growing Sideways in the Twentieth Century* (Durham, NC: Duke University Press, 2009).

### CHAPTER FOUR. TRANS* GENERATIONS

1. *Paris Is Burning*, dir. Jennie Livingston (Miramax Films, 1990).

2. Marlon Bailey, *Butch Queens Up in Pumps: Gender Performance and Ballroom Culture in Detriot* (Ann Arbor: University of Michigan Press, 2013).

3. Chandan Reddy, "Houses, Homes, Non-Identity: *Paris Is Burning*," in *Burning Down the House: Recycling Domesticity*, edited by Rosemary Marangoly George, 355–79 (Boulder, CO: Westview Press, 1998).

4. See, e.g., Esther Newton, "My Best Informant's Dress: The Erotic Equation in Fieldwork," *Cultural Anthropology* 8, no. 1(1993): 3–23; Kath Weston, *Families We Choose: Lesbians, Gays, Kinship* (New York: Columbia University Press, 2005).

5. Bailey, *Butch Queens Up in Pumps*, 80.

6. Tey Meadow, "The Child," *TSQ: Transgender Studies Quarterly* 1, nos. 1–2 (2014): 57.

7. Ibid.

8. Ibid.

9. Marilyn Strathern, *After Nature: English Kinship in the Late Twentieth Century* (Cambridge: Cambridge University Press, 1992).

10. Del LaGrace Volcano, *Sublime Mutations* (Berlin: Janssen, 2004).

11. J.R. Latham, "(Re)Making Sex: A Praxiography of The Gender Clinic," *Feminist Theory* (March 2017); PDF available at http://journals. sagepub.com/doi/pdf/10.1177/1464700117700051.

12. Sara Davidmann, *Ken. To Be Destroyed* (Amsterdam: Schilt Publishing, 2016).

13. Marianne Hirsch, comp., *Family Frames: Photography, Narrative, and Postmemory* (Cambridge, MA: Harvard University Press, 1997), 13.

14. Maggie Nelson, *The Argonauts* (Minneapolis: Graywolf Press, 2015), 83.

15. Saidiya Hartman, "Venus in Two Acts," *small axe*, 26th ser., 12, no. 2 (June 2008): 1–14.

16. www.tgijp.com.

17. Jayden Donahue, "Making It Happen, Mama: A Conversation with Miss Major," in *Captive Genders: Trans Embodiment and the Prison Industrial Complex*, expanded 2nd ed., edited by Eric A. Stanley and Nat Smith (Oakland, CA: AK Press, 2015), 277.

18. Sarah Haley, *No Mercy Here: Gender, Punishment, and the Making of Jim Crow Modernity* (Chapel Hill: University of North Carolina Press, 2016).

19. Lori Girshick, "Out of Compliance: Masculine-Identified People in Women's Prisons," in Stanley and Smith (eds.), *Captive Genders*, 196.

20. Kristopher Shelley "Krystal," "Krystal Is Kristopher and Vice Versa," in Stanley and Smith (eds.), *Captive Genders*, 167.

21. Ibid., 167–70.

22. Morgan Bassichis, Alexander Lee, and Dean Spade, "Building an Abolitionist Trans and Queer Movement with Everything We've Got," in Stanley and Smith (eds.), *Captive Genders*, 37.

23. José Esteban Muñoz, *Cruising Utopia: The Then and There of Queer Futurity* (New York: NYU Press, 2009), 11, 22.

24. Bassichis, Lee, and Spade, "Building an Abolitionist Trans and Queer Movement," 37.

CHAPTER FIVE. TRANS* REPRESENTATION

1. Elizabeth Freeman, introduction to *Time Binds: Queer Temporalities, Queer Histories*. (Durham, NC: Duke University Press, 2010), xi.

2. Lee Edelman, *No Future: Queer Theory and the Death Drive* (Durham, NC: Duke University Press, 2004).

3. José Esteban Muõz, *Cruising Utopia: The Then and There of Queer Futurity* (New York: NYU Press, 2009).

4. Kara Keeling, "Looking for M——: Queer Temporality, Black Political Possibility, and Poetry from the Future," *GLQ: A Journal of Les-*

*bian and Gay Studies* 15, no. 4 (2009): 565–82; Tavia Nyong'o, "Do You Want Queer Theory (or Do You Want the Truth)? Intersections of Punk and Queer in the 1970s," *Radical History Review*, no. 100 (Winter 2008): 103–19.

5. Sandy Stone, "The 'Empire' Strikes Back: A Posttransexual Manifesto," in *Body Guards: The Cultural Politics of Sexual Ambiguity*, edited by Julia Epstein and Kristina Straub (New York: Routledge, 1992), 280–304. Stone refers here to Gary Kates, "D'Éon Returns to France: Gender and Power in 1777," in Epstein and Straub (eds.), *Body Guards*, 167–94, and probably to an early version of ethnographic work by Anne Bolin on transgender people in the Midwest, "Traversing Gender: Cultural Context and Gender Practices," in *Gender Reversals and Gender Cultures: Anthropological and Historical Perspectives*, edited by Sabrina Petra Ramet (London: Routledge, 1996), 22–51.

6. Jeanne Vacarro, "Handmade," *TSQ: Transgender Studies Quarterly* 1, nos. 1–2 (2014): 96–97.

7. Laura Marks, *Touch: Sensuous Media and Multisensory Media* (Minneapolis: University of Minnesota Press, 2002), 20.

8. http://harrydodge.com.

9. Sarah Sulistio, interview with Harry Dodge, *Miami Rail*, Spring 2017, http://miamirail.org/performing-arts/harry-dodge.

10. See, e.g., Linzi Juliano, "Becoming Transreal: Micha Cárdenas and Elle Mehrmand mix first life with Second Life," *CSW Update* (UCLA Center for the Study of Women Newsletter), December 2010, available at http://escholarship.org/uc/item/76b8b02k.

11. Jack Halberstam, "The Transgender Gaze in *Boys Don't Cry*," *Screen* 42, no. 3 (Autumn 2001): 294–98.

12. On transnormalization, see, e.g., Jin Haritaworn and Riley Snorton, "Trans Necropolitics," in *The Transgender Studies Reader 2*, edited by Aren Aizura and Susan Stryker (New York: Routledge, 2013), 66–76; and Jasbir Puar, "Bodies with New Organs Becoming Trans, Becoming Disabled," *Social Text* 33, no. 3 (September 2015): 45–73. On the materiality of grammar, see Mel Y. Chen, *Animacies: Biopolitics, Racial Mattering, and Queer Affect* (Durham, NC: Duke University Press, 2012). And on somatechnics, see Nikki Sullivan, "Somatechnics," *Transgender Studies Quarterly* 1, nos. 1–2 (2014): 187–90.

13. Kory Grow, "'Transparent' Creator Jill Soloway Making the World Safe for Trans People," *Rolling Stone,* October 20, 2014, www .rollingstone.com/tv/features/transparent-jill-soloway-20141020; Stacy Lambe, "The Bi-Curious Case of Amy Landecker," *OUT Magazine,* October 14, 2014; Diane Anderson-Minshall, "Amazon's *Transparent* Is Great Television in Transition," *Advocate,* September 11, 2014, www.advocate.com/arts-entertainment/television/2014/09/11/amazons-transparent-great-television-transition.

14. Julie Miller, "*Transparent*'s Jeffrey Tambor Says He Wants to Be the Last Cisgender Actor in a Trans Role," *Vanity Fair,* September 18, 2016, www.vanityfair.com/hollywood/2016/09/emmys-transparent-jeffrey-tambor-cis-trans-actors.

15. See, e.g., Chandan Reddy, *Freedom with Violence: Race, Sexuality, and the U.S. State* (Durham, NC: Duke University Press, 2011); and Etienne Balibar, *Violence and Civility: On the Limits of Political Philosophy* (New York: Columbia University Press, 2016).

## CHAPTER SIX. TRANS* FEMINISM

1. Janice Raymond, *The Transsexual Empire: The Making of the She-Male* (1979; New York: Teachers College Press, 1994).

2. See, e.g., Sheila Jeffreys, *The Lesbian Heresy* (New York: Spinifex Press, 1993); and Mary Daly, *Gyn/Ecology: The Metaethics of Radical Feminism* (Boston: Beacon Press, 1990), both arguing for a very narrow understanding of the category of "woman." Andrea Dworkin, in contrast, supported more flexible notions of gender; see, e.g., *Woman Hating* (New York: Plume, 1991).

3. Raymond, *Transsexual Empire,* 104.

4. Sheila Jeffreys, "Transgender Activism: A Lesbian Feminist Perspective," *Journal of Lesbian Studies* 1, nos. 3–4 (1997).

5. For an affirmative account of the affective pull of this festival for lesbian feminists, see Jill Dolan, "Feeling Women's Culture: Women's Music, Lesbian Feminism, and the Impact of Emotional Memory," keynote address, "Resoundingly Queer" conference, Cornell University, April 1, 2012; published online at the *Feminist Spectator:* https://feministspectator.princeton.edu/lectures-2/feeling-womens-culture.

6. Julia Serano, *Whipping Girl: A Transsexual Woman on Sexism and the Scapegoating of Femininity* (Berkeley, CA: Seal Press, 2007).

7. Leslie Feinberg, *Stone Butch Blues* (Ithaca, NY: Firebrand Books, 1993).

8. Mike Curie, "The Nature and Treatment of Transsexualism: When a Woman Becomes a Man," *Echo of Sappho*, no. 5 (Summer/Fall 1973): 14.

9. *Echo of Sappho*, no. 5 (Summer/Fall 1973): 17.

10. Ibid., 18.

11. Catherine Crouch, "Films: The Genderactor," 2016 (article accessed at www.catherinecrouch.com; no longer available).

12. Susan Stryker, "Sign the Petition to Stop a Transphobic Film in Frameline LGBT Film Festival," *Left in SF,* May 23, 2007. (Article accessed online: http://archive.is/Nznc. No longer available in full form.)

13. Serano, *Whipping Girl,* 341.

14. Julia Serano, "Gender Is Not Just a Performance," *Jezebel,* September 24, 2010, http://jezebel.com/5647120/gender-is-not-just-a-performance.

15. Jay Prosser, *Second Skins: Body Narratives of Transsexuality* (New York: Columbia University Press, 1998); Vivianne Namaste, *Invisible Lives: The Erasure of Transsexual and Transgendered People* (Chicago: University of Chicago Press, 2000); Henry Rubin, *Self-Made Men: Identity and Embodiment among Transsexual Men* (Nashville, TN: Vanderbilt University Press, 2003); Stephen Whittle, *The Transgender Debate: The Crisis Surrounding Gender Identity* (New York: Ithaca Press, 2001).

16. Prosser, *Second Skins,* 32.

17. J.R. Latham, "(Re)Making Sex: A Praxiography of the Gender Clinic," *Feminist Theory,* March 2017; idem, "Trans Men's Sexual Narrative-Practices: Introducing STS to Trans and Sexuality Studies," *Sexualities* 19, no. 3 (2016): 347–68; and Micha Cárdenas, "Becoming Dragon: A Transversal Technology Study," in *Code Drift: Essays in Critical Digital Studies,* edited by Arthur and Marilouise Kroker (Victoria, BC: Pacific Centre for Technology and Culture, 2010), 127–52; available online at www.ctheory.net/articles.aspx?id=639.

18. Lisa M. Diamond, *Sexual Fluidity: Understanding Women's Love and Desire* (Cambridge, MA: Harvard University Press, 2009).

19. Judith Butler, *Gender Trouble: Feminism and the Subversion of Identity* (New York: Routledge, 1990).

20. Judith Butler, *Bodies That Matter: On Discursive Limits of Sex* (New York: Routledge, 1993).

21. Judith Butler, *Undoing Gender* (New York: Routledge, 2004), 28.

22. Paisley Currah, "General Editor's Introduction," *TSQ: Transgender Studies Quarterly* 3, nos. 1–2 (May 2016): 2.

23. Susan Stryker and Talia M. Bettcher, "Introduction: Trans/Feminisms," *TSQ: Transgender Studies Quarterly* 3, nos. 1–2 (May 2016): 6.

24. Kimberle Crenshaw, "Mapping the Margins: Intersectionality, Identity Politics, and Violence against Women of Color," *Stanford Law Review* 43, no. 6 (July 1991): 1241–99.

25. Ibid., quoting Rivera's speech at a 1973 Liberation Day rally in Washington Square, New York.

26. Claudia Sofía Garriga-López, "Transfeminist Crossroads: Reimagining the Ecuadorian State," *TSQ: Transgender Studies Quarterly* 3, nos. 1–2 (May 2016): 105.

27. Ibid., 107.

28. Eva Hayward, "Spider City Sex," *Women & Performance: A Journal of Feminist Theory* 20, no. 3 (November 2010): 229.

29. Ibid., 226.

## CONCLUSIONS

1. English translation of the Danish phrase *leg godt,* from which the term "Lego" was taken.

2. "Learn to Speak LEGO: BASIC TERMS," http://thebrickblogger.com/2010/11/lego-disctionary-basic-term.

3. "Lego Glossary," www.brothers-brick.com/lego-glossary.

4. Lucas Cassidy Crawford, "Breaking Ground on a Theory of Transgender Architecture," *Seattle Journal for Social Justice* 8, no. 2 (2010): 517.

5. See Sheila Cavanagh, *Queering Bathrooms: Gender, Sexuality, and the Hygienic Imagination* (Toronto: University of Toronto Press, 2010), for a psychoanalytic take on bathroom dynamics.

6. Gayle Salamon, *Assuming a Body: Transgender and Rhetorics of Materiality* (New York: Columbia University Press, 2010).

7. Stefano Harney and Fred Moten, *The Undercommons: Fugitive Planning and Black Study* (Durham, NC: Duke University Press, 2013); available at www.minorcompositions.info/wp-content/uploads/2013 /04/undercommons-web.pdf.

# ON PRONOUNS

Every few weeks, I get an email from a colleague, a friend, or a student asking me what pronoun I prefer. By way of preamble: I mostly go by "Jack" nowadays, although people who have known me for a really long time and some family members still call me Judith. Then there are a few people, my sister included, who call me "Jude." I have debated switching out Jack for Jude to try to compress the name ambiguity into a more clear opposition between Judith and Jude. But then again—and contrary to my personality or my politics—when it comes to names and pronouns, I am a bit of a free floater. This goes against my instincts and my general demeanor—I don't hang in the middle ground on much, not politically, not socially, not in terms of culture, queer issues, feminism or masculinity. I am a person of strong opinions, so why, oh why, do I insist on being loosey goosey about pronouns?

Well, a few reasons: First, I have not transitioned in any formal sense, and certainly there are many differences between my gender and those of transgender men on hormones. Second, the back and forth between he and she sort of captures the form that my gender takes nowadays. Not that I am often an unambiguous "she," but neither am I often an unambiguous "he." Third, I think my floating gender pronouns capture well the refusal to resolve my gender ambiguity, which itself has become a kind of identity for me.

I watch friends, one after the other, transition, mostly from butch to TG male, and I wonder whether I am just sitting on a fence and not wanting to jump. But actually, as a real medi-phobe, I don't see taking hormones, even in small doses, as right for me for any extended amount of time. Top surgery? Well, yes please, I did that, but it has made it even harder for me to use the women's locker room when I swim or work out. So while I could "transition" and still live in the ever-evolving, improvised territory of transgenderism ... I prefer not to.

Like Bartleby, that wonderful and doleful example of a refusenik who declined to explain his refusal to work, to comply, to communicate even, I prefer not to transition in any way that would understand it as a process with a destination; rather, like so many of the theorists I reference in this book, I think of myself as perpetually in transition. I prefer not to clarify what must categorically remain murky. I prefer not to help people out in their gender quandaries, and yet, I appreciate you asking.

I still use women's restrooms, and I avoid any and all contact on going in or coming out. If someone looks frightened when they see me, I say, "Excuse me," and allow my "fluty" voice to gender me. If someone looks angry, I turn away. But mostly I just ignore what is going on around me in the restroom and do what I am there to do. I wish more people would behave like my partner's son and simply ask, politely and without judgment, what pronoun an individual prefers—he rarely presumes and often asks. I also wish more people would use a pronoun system based on gender and not on sex, based on comfort rather than biology, based on the presumption that there are many gendered bodies in the world and "male" and "female" do not even begin the hard work of classifying them.

So, if you are wondering about my pronoun use and would like it resolved once and for all, I cannot help you there. But if, like the UK in the 1980s, you are ready to give up on the "imperial" system of measurements in favor of new metrics, then consider my gender improvised at best, uncertain and mispronounced more often than not, irresolvable and ever shifting. And P.S.: grouping me with someone else who seems to have a female embodiment and then calling us "LADIES" is never, ever, okay!

# WORKS CITED

Agamben, Giorgio. *Homo Sacer: Sovereign Power and Bare Life.* Translated by Daniel Heller-Roazen. Palo Alto, CA: Stanford University Press, 1998.

Aizura, Aren Z. "The Romance of the Amazing Scalpel: 'Race,' Labour, and Affect in Thai Gender Reassignment Clinics." In *Queer Bangkok: 21st-Century Markets, Media, and Rights,* edited by Peter Jackson, 144–62. Hong Kong: Hong Kong University Press, 2011.

*The Aggressives.* Directed by Eric Daniel Peddle. 2005.

Anderson-Minshall, Diane. "Amazon's *Transparent* Is Great Television in Transition." *Advocate,* September 11, 2014, www.advocate.com /arts-entertainment/television/2014/09/11/amazons-transparent-great-television-transition.

Bailey, Marlon. *Butch Queens Up in Pumps: Gender, Performance, and Ballroom Culture in Detroit.* Ann Arbor: University of Michigan Press, 2013.

Balibar, Etienne. *Violence and Civility: On the Limits of Political Philosophy.* New York: Columbia University Press, 2016.

Bassichis, Morgan, Alexander Lee, and Dean Spade. "Building an Abolitionist Trans and Queer Movement with Everything We've Got." In *Captive Genders: Trans Embodiment and the Prison Industrial*

*Complex,* expanded 2nd ed., edited by Eric A. Stanley and Nat Smith, 15–40. Oakland, CA: AK Press, 2015.

Beauchamp, Toby. "Artful Concealment and Strategic Visibility: Transgender Bodies and U.S. State Surveillance after 9/11." In *The Transgender Studies Reader 2,* edited by Aren Aizura and Susan Stryker, 46–55. New York: Routledge, 2013.

Beckett, Samuel. *The Unnamable.* New York: Grove Press, 1958.

Bederman, Gail. *Manliness and Civilization: A Cultural History of Gender and Race in the United States, 1880–1917.* Chicago: University of Chicago Press, 1995.

Bolin, Anne. "Traversing Gender: Cultural Context and Gender Practices." In *Gender Reversals and Gender Cultures: Anthropological and Historical Perspectives,* edited by Sabrina Petra Ramet, 22–51. London: Routledge, 1996.

*Boys Don't Cry.* Directed by Kimberly Peirce. Fox Searchlight Pictures, 1999.

Butler, Judith. *Bodies That Matter: On Discursive Limits of Sex.* New York: Routledge, 1993.

———. *Gender Trouble: Feminism and the Subversion of Identity.* New York: Routledge, 1990.

———. *Undoing Gender.* New York: Routledge, 2004.

*By Hook or by Crook.* Directed by Harry Dodge and Silas Howard. Steakhaus Productions, 2001.

Cárdenas, Micha. "Becoming Dragon: A Transversal Technology Study." In *Code Drift: Essays in Critical Digital Studies,* edited by Arthur and Marilouise Kroker, 127–52. Victoria, BC: Pacific Centre for Technology and Culture, 2010. Available online at www.ctheory.net/articles.aspx?id=639.

Cavanagh, Sheila. *Queering Bathrooms: Gender, Sexuality, and the Hygienic Imagination.* Toronto: University of Toronto Press, 2010.

Chen, Mel Y. *Animacies: Biopolitics, Racial Mattering, and Queer Affect.* Durham, NC: Duke University Press, 2012.

Cotton, Tristan. *Hung Jury: Testimonies of Genital Surgery by Transsexual Men.* San Francisco: Transgress Press, 2012.

Crawford, Lucas Cassidy. "Breaking Ground on a Theory of Transgender Architecture." *Seattle Journal for Social Justice* 8, no. 2

(2010): 515–39. Available at digitalcommons.law.seattleu.edu/sjsj/vol8/iss2/5/.

Crenshaw, Kimberle. "Mapping the Margins: Intersectionality, Identity Politics, and Violence against Women of Color." *Stanford Law Review* 43, no. 6 (July 1991): 1241–99.

Crouch, Catherine. "Films: The Gendercator." 2006. www.catherinecrouch.com. (Article no longer available.) See also https://en.wikipedia.org/wiki/Catherine_Crouch.

*The Crying Game.* Directed by Neil Jordan. Palace Pictures, 1992.

Curie, Mike. "The Nature and Treatment of Transsexualism: When a Woman Becomes a Man." *Echo of Sappho*, no. 5 (Summer/Fall 1973): 14.

Currah, Paisley. "General Editor's Introduction." *TSQ: Transgender Studies Quarterly*, "Trans/Feminisms" special issue, 3, nos. 1–2 (May 2016): 1–4.

Daly, Mary. *Gyn/Ecology: The Metaethics of Radical Feminism.* Boston: Beacon Press, 1990.

Davidmann, Sara. *Ken. To Be Destroyed.* Amsterdam: Schilt Publishing, 2016.

Deleuze, Gilles, and Félix Guattari. *Anti-Oedipus: Capitalism and Schizophrenia.* Translated by Robert Hurly, Mark Seem, and Helen R. Lane. Minneapolis: University of Minnesota Press, 1983.

*Diagnostic and Statistical Manuel of Mental Disorders.* 2nd and 5th editions. Washington DC: American Psychiatric Association, 1968 and 2013.

Dickens, Charles. *Great Expectations.* 1860; Peterborough, Ont.: Broadview Press, 1998.

Dillon, Michael. *Self: A Study in Endocrinlogy and Ethics.* 1946; Oxford: Butterworth-Heinemann, 2013.

Dolan, Jill. "Feeling Women's Culture: Women's Music, Lesbian Feminism, and the Impact of Emotional Memory." Keynote address, "Resoundingly Queer" conference, Cornell University, April 1, 2012. Published online at the *Feminist Spectator*, https://feministspectator.princeton.edu/lectures-2/feeling-womens-culture.

Donahue, Jayden. "Making It Happen, Mama: A Conversation with Miss Major." In *Captive Genders: Trans Embodiment and the Prison Industrial Complex*, expanded 2nd ed., edited by Eric A. Stanley and Nat Smith, 267–80. Oakland, CA: AK Press, 2015.

Dworkin, Andrea. *Woman Hating.* New York: Plume, 1991.

Edelman, Lee. *No Future: Queer Theory and the Death Drive.* Durham, NC: Duke University Press, 2004.

Ellison, Ralph. *Invisible Man.* New York: Random House, 1952.

El-Tayeb, Fatima. *European Others: Queering Ethnicity in Postnational Europe.* Minneapolis: University of Minnesota Press, 2011.

Feinberg, Leslie. *Stone Butch Blues.* Ithaca, NY: Firebrand Books, 1993.

Ferguson, Roderick A. *Aberrations in Black: Toward a Queer of Color Critique.* Minneapolis: University of Minnesota Press, 2003.

*Finding Nemo.* Directed by Andrew Stanton. Buena Vista Pictures, 2003.

Foucault, Michel. *History of Sexuality,* vol. 1: *An Introduction.* Translated by Robert Hurley. New York: Random House, 1978.

Freeman, Elizabeth. *Time Binds: Queer Temporalities, Queer Histories.* Durham, NC: Duke University Press, 2010.

*Fremde Haut.* Directed by Angelina Maccarone. 2005.

Garriga-López, Claudia Sofía. "Transfeminist Crossroads: Reimagining the Ecuadorian State," *TSQ: Transgender Studies Quarterly* 3, nos. 1–2 (May 2016): 104–19.

Freud, Sigmund. *Three Essays on the Theory of Sexuality* (1905). Translated by James Strachey. New York: Basic Books, 2000.

Girshick, Lori. "Out of Compliance: Masculine-Identified People in Women's Prisons." In *Captive Genders: Trans Embodiment and the Prison Industrial Complex,* expanded 2nd ed., edited by Eric A. Stanley and Nat Smith, 189–208. Oakland, CA: AK Press, 2015.

Griggs, Claudine. *Passage to Trinidad.* 1996; London: Bloomsbury Academic, 2005.

Grow, Kory. "'Transparent' Creator Jill Soloway Making the World Safe for Trans People." *Rolling Stone,* October 20, 2014, www.rollingstone.com/tv/features/transparent-jill-soloway-20141020.

Halberstam, J. Jack. *In a Queer Time and Place: Transgender Bodies, Subcultural Lives.* New York: NYU Press, 2015.

———. "The Transgender Gaze in *Boys Don't Cry.*" *Screen* 42, no. 3 (Autumn 2001): 294–98.

Halberstam, Judith. *Female Masculinity.* Durham, NC: Duke University Press, 1998.

Haley, Sarah. *No Mercy Here: Gender, Punishment, and the Making of Jim Crow Modernity.* Chapel Hill: University of North Carolina Press, 2016.

Hall, Radclyffe. *The Well of Loneliness.* Garden City, NY: Sun Dial Press, 1928.

Hanssmann, Christoph. "Passing Torches: Feminist Inquiries and Trans-Health Politics and Practices." *TSQ: Transgender Studies Quarterly* 3, nos. 1–2 (May 2016): 120–36.

Haritawarn, Jin, and Riley Snorton. "Trans Necropolitics." In *The Transgender Studies Reader 2,* edited by Aren Aizura and Susan Stryker, 66–76. New York: Routledge, 2013.

Harney, Stefano, and Fred Moten. *The Undercommons: Fugitive Planning and Black Study.* Durham, NC: Duke University Press, 2013. Available at www.minorcompositions.info/wp-content/uploads/2013/04/undercommons-web.pdf.

Hartman, Saidiya. "Venus in Two Acts." *small axe,* 26th ser., 12, no. 2 (2008): 1–14.

Hayward, Eva. "Spider City Sex." *Women & Performance: A Journal of Feminist Theory* 20, no. 3 (November 2010): 225–51.

Hayward, Eva, and Jami Weinstein. "Introduction: Tranimalities in the Age of Trans* Life." *TSQ: Transgender Studies Quarterly* 2, no. 2 (May 2015): 195–208.

Hirsch, Marianne, comp. *Family Frames: Photography, Narrative, and Postmemory.* Cambridge, MA: Harvard University Press, 1997.

Jeffreys, Sheila. *The Lesbian Heresy.* New York: Spinifex Press, 1993.

———. "Transgender Activism: A Lesbian Feminist Perspective." *Journal of Lesbian Studies* 1, nos. 3–4 (1997).

Juliano, Linzi. "Becoming Transreal: Micha Cárdenas and Elle Mehrmand mix first life with Second Life." *CSW Update* (UCLA Center for the Study of Women Newsletter), December 2010. Available at http://escholarship.org/uc/item/76b8b02k.

Kafka, Franz. *The Metamorphosis.* Edited by Stanley Corngold. Toronto: Bantam Books, 1981.

Kates, Gary. "D'Éon Returns to France: Gender and Power in 1777." In *Body Guards: The Cultural Politics of Sexual Ambiguity,* edited by Julia Epstein and Kristina Straub, 167–94. New York: Routledge, 1992.

————. *Monsieur d'Éon Is a Woman: A Tale of Political Intrigue and Sexual Masquerade.* Baltimore: Johns Hopkins University Press, 1995.

Keeling, Kara. "Looking for M————: Queer Temporality, Black Political Possibility, and Poetry from the Future." *GLQ: A Journal of Lesbian and Gay Studies* 15, no. 4 (2009): 565–82.

Kennedy, Pagan. *The First Man-Made Man: The Story of Two Sex Changes, One Love Affair, and a Twentieth-Century Medical Revolution.* London: Bloomsbury, 2007.

Krafft-Ebing, Richard von. *Psychopathia Sexualis, with Special Reference to Contrary Sexual Instinct: A Medico-Legal Study.* Philadelphia: F.A. Davis Co., 1886. Available at archive.org/details/psychopathia sexoochadgoog.

Kreps, Daniel. "Prince Warns Young Artists: Record Contracts Are 'Slavery.'" *Rolling Stone,* August 9, 2015. www.rollingstone.com/music /news/prince-warns-young-artists-record-contracts-are-slavery-20150809.

Lambe, Stacy. "The Bi-Curious Case of Amy Landecker." *OUT Magazine,* October 14, 2014.

Latham, J.R. "(Re)Making Sex: A Praxiography of the Gender Clinic." *Feminist Theory,* March 2017. PDF available at http://journals .sagepub.com/doi/pdf/10.1177/1464700117700051.

————. "Trans Men's Sexual Narrative-Practices: Introducing STS to Trans and Sexuality Studies." *Sexualities* 19, no. 3 (2016): 347–68.

*The Lego Movie.* Directed by Phil Lord and Chris Miller. Warner Brothers, 2014.

Levy, Ariel. "Dolls and Feelings." *New Yorker,* December 14, 2015. www .newyorker.com/magazine/2015/12/14/dolls-and-feelings.

Lombroso, Cesare, and William Ferrero. *The Female Offender.* New York: D. Appleton & Co., 1898.

Marks, Laura. *Touch: Sensuous Media and Multisensory Media.* Minneapolis: University of Minnesota Press, 2002.

Martínez, María Elena. "Archives, Bodies, and Imagination: The Case of Juana Aguilar and Queer Approaches to History, Sexuality, and Politics." *Radical History Review,* no. 120 (Fall 2014): 159–82.

*Ma Vie en Rose.* Directed by Alain Berliner. Haut et Court, 1997.

McBee, Thomas Page. *Man Alive: A True Story of Violence, Forgiveness, and Becoming a Man.* San Francisco: City Lights/Sister Spit, 2014.

McKenna, Wendy, and Suzanne J. Kessler. *Gender: An Ethnomethodological Approach.* Chicago: University of Chicago Press, 1985.

Meadow, Tey. "The Child." *TSQ: Transgender Study Quarterly* 1, nos. 1–2 (2014): 57–59.

Melville, Herman. *Moby Dick.* London: Constable & Co., 1922.

Meyerowitz, Joanne. "America's Original Transgender Sweetheart." *Politico Magazine,* June 16, 2015. www.politico.com/magazine/story /2015/06/caitlyn-jenner-was-not-americas-first-transgender-sweetheart-christine-jorgensen-119080.

Miller, Julie. "*Transparent*'s Jeffrey Tambor Says He Wants to Be the Last Cisgender Actor in a Trans Role." *Vanity Fair,* September 18, 2016, www.vanityfair.com/hollywood/2016/09/emmys-transparent-jeffrey-tambor-cis-trans-actors.

*Monty Python's Life of Brian.* Directed by Terry Jones. Cinema International Corporation (UK), Orion Pictures/Warner Bros (US), 1979.

Morgensen, Scott Lauria. *Spaces between Us: Queer Settler Colonialism and Indigenous Decolonization.* Minneapolis: University of Minnesota Press, 2011.

Muñoz, José Esteban. *Cruising Utopia: The Then and There of Queer Futurity.* New York: NYU Press, 2009.

Najmabadi, Afsaneh. *Professing Selves: Transsexuality and Same-Sex Desire in Contemporary Iran (Experimental Futures).* Durham, NC: Duke University Press, 2014.

Namaste, Vivianne. *Invisible Lives: The Erasure of Transsexual and Transgendered People.* Chicago: University of Chicago Press, 2000.

National Center for Transgender Equality. "About Us." 2017. www .transequality.org/about.

Nelson, Maggie. *The Argonauts.* Minneapolis: Graywolf Press, 2015.

Nyong'o, Tavia. "Do You Want Queer Theory (or Do You Want the Truth)? Intersections of Punk and Queer in the 1970s." *Radical History Review,* no. 100 (Winter 2008): 103–19.

*Paper Dolls (Bubot Niyar).* Directed by Tomer Heymann. Strand Releasing, 2006.

*Paris Is Burning*. Directed by Jennie Livingston. Miramax Films, 1990.

Perry, Wynne. "Gender Dysphoria: DSM-5 Reflects Shift In Perspective on Gender Identity." *Huffington Post*, June 4, 2013. www.huffingtonpost .com/2013/06/04/gender-dysphoria-dsm-5_n_3385287.html.

Preciado, Paul B. *Pornotopia: An Essay on Playboy's Architecture and Biopolitics*. Cambridge, MA: MIT Press/Zone Books, 2014.

————. *Testo Junkie: Sex, Drugs, and Biopolitics in the Pharmacopornographic Era* (2008). Translated from the French by Bruce Benderson. New York: Feminist Press at the City University of New York, 2013.

Prosser, Jay. *Second Skins: Body Narratives of Transsexuality*. New York: Columbia University Press, 1998.

Puar, Jasbir. "Bodies with New Organs Becoming Trans, Becoming Disabled." *Social Text* 33, no. 3 (September 2015): 45–73.

Raymond, Janice. *The Transsexual Empire: The Making of the She-Male*. 1979; New York: Teachers College Press, 1994.

Reddy, Chandan. *Freedom with Violence: Race, Sexuality, and the U.S. State*. Durham, NC: Duke University Press, 2011.

————. "Houses, Homes, Non-Identity: *Paris Is Burning*." In *Burning Down the House: Recycling Domesticity*, edited by Rosemary Marangoly George, 355–79. Boulder, CO: Westview Press, 1998.

Rubin, Gayle. "The Traffic in Women: Notes on the 'Political Economy' of Sex" (1975). In *The Second Wave: A Reader in Feminist Theory*, edited by Linda Nicholson, 27–62. New York: Routledge, 1997.

Rubin, Henry. *Self-Made Men: Identity and Embodiment among Transsexual Men*. Nashville, TN: Vanderbilt University Press, 2003.

Rushdie, Salman. *Midnight's Children*. 1981; New York: Random House, 2006.

Salamon, Gayle. *Assuming a Body: Transgender and Rhetorics of Materiality*. New York: Columbia University Press, 2010.

Serano, Julia. "Gender Is Not Just a Performance." *Jezebel*, September 24, 2010, http://jezebel.com/5647120/gender-is-not-just-a-performance.

————. *Whipping Girl: A Transsexual Woman on Sexism and the Scapegoating of Femininity*. Berkeley, CA: Seal Press, 2007.

Shelley, Kristopher "Krystal." "Krystal Is Kristopher and Vice Versa." In *Captive Genders: Trans Embodiment and the Prison Industrial Complex*, expanded 2nd ed., edited by Eric A. Stanley and Nat Smith, 191–94. Oakland, CA: AK Press, 2015.

Snorton, Riley. *Black on Both Sides: A Racial History of Trans Identity.* Minneapolis: University of Minnesota Press, 2017.

Spade, Dean. *Normal Life: Administrative Violence, Critical Trans Politics, and the Limits of Law.* Durham, NC: Duke University Press, 2011.

Spillers, Hortense J. "Mama's Baby, Papa's Maybe: An American Grammar Book." *Diacritics* 17, no. 2 (Summer 1987): 64–81.

Stallings, L. H. *Funk the Erotic: Transaesthetics and Black Sexual Cultures.* Champaign: University of Illinois Press, 2015.

Stanley, Eric A., and Nat Smith, eds. *Captive Genders: Trans Embodiment and the Prison Industrial Complex.* Expanded 2nd ed. Oakland, CA: AK Press, 2015.

Stockton, Kathryn Bond. *The Queer Child, or Growing Sideways in the Twentieth Century.* Durham, NC: Duke University Press, 2009.

Stone, Sandy. "The 'Empire' Strikes Back: A Posttransexual Manifesto." In *Body Guards: The Cultural Politics of Sexual Ambiguity,* edited by Julia Epstein and Kristina Straub, 280–304. New York: Routledge, 1992.

Strathern, Marilyn. *After Nature: English Kinship in the Late Twentieth Century.* Cambridge: Cambridge University Press, 1992.

Stryker, Susan. "Sign the Petition to Stop a Transphobic Film in Frameline LGBT Film Festival." *Left in SF,* May 23, 2007. (Article accessed online: http://archive.is/Nznc. No longer available in full form.)

Stryker, Susan, and Talia M. Bettcher. "Introduction: Trans /Feminisms." *TSQ: Transgender Studies Quarterly,* Trans/Feminisms special issue, 3, nos. 1–2 (May 2016): 5–14.

Sullivan, Nikki. "Somatechnics." *Transgender Studies Quarterly* 1, nos. 1–2 (2014): 187–90.

Sylvia Rivera Law Project (SRLP). "About SRLP." 2017. https://srlp.org/about.

*Tangerine.* Directed by Sean Baker. Magnolia Pictures, 2015.

Taylor, Fredrick Winslow. *The Principles of Scientific Management.* New York: Harper & Bros., 1911. Available at archive.org/details /principlesofscie1911tayl.

*Tomboy.* Directed by Céline Sciamma. Pyramide Distribution, 2011.

*Transparent.* Created and directed by Jill Soloway. Amazon Studios, 2014

Vacarro, Jeanne. "Feelings and Fractals: Woolly Ecologies of Transgender Matter." *GLQ: A Journal of Lesbian and Gay Studies* 21, nos. 2–3 (2015): 273–93.

———. "Handmade." *TSQ: Transgender Studies Quarterly* 1, nos. 1–2 (2014): 96–97.

Valentine, David. *Imagining Transgender: An Ethnography of a Category.* Durham, NC: Duke University Press, 2007.

Velasco, Sherry. *The Lieutenant Nun: Transgenderism, Lesbian Desire, and Catalina de Erauso.* Austin: University of Texas Press, 2000.

Volcano, Del LaGrace. *Sublime Mutations.* Berlin: Janssen, 2000.

Whittle, Stephen. *The Transgender Debate.* New York: Ithaca Press, 2001.